LONDON'S LOST DEPARTMENT STORES

The daintiest
of Leg-Wear
at
DERRY
& TOMS

F GREGORY
BROWN B

Tessa Boase is a former *Daily Telegraph* journalist and
author of *The Housekeeper's Tale* ('A fluent study . . .
a deep, rich account of their individual lives',
Times Literary Supplement) and *Etta Lemon: The Woman
Who Saved the Birds* ('Dazzling', *Daily Telegraph*).

tessaboase.com   @tessaboase

Tessa Boase

LONDON'S LOST DEPARTMENT STORES

A VANISHED WORLD OF DAZZLE AND DREAMS

SAFE HAVEN

First published in 2022 by Safe Haven Books Ltd
12 Chinnocks Wharf
42 Narrow Street
London E14 8DJ
www.safehavenbooks.co.uk

A catalogue record for this book is available from the
British Library.

ISBN 978 1 8384051 3 7

10 9 8 7 6 5 4 3 2 1

The Safe Haven team on *London's Lost Department
Stores*: Tessa Boase, Nick Glass, Graham Coster, Tim
Peters and David Welch

Designed and typeset in Anna ITC and Brandon by
TimPetersDesign.co.uk

Printed and bound in the EU by GraphyCems

Acknowledgements

The subject of department stores seems to act as an instant trigger, unleashing reminiscences, arcane knowledge and tales of family connections. I've enjoyed hearing them all. Particular thanks to: Mieke Hille for sharing Maggi Giles's 1958 scrapbook of D. H. Evans; Pamela Kingsford for the image of her mother Esme Bradburne, plantswoman for Derry & Toms' roof garden; Glyn Hatfield for his junk shop album of Morgan Squire in Leicester; Sherry Garlick Stanton, great-granddaughter and chronicler of Garlicks department stores of South Africa, and John Marwood, historian of Stuttafords of South Africa; Julia Ball and Edward Hill, great-grandchildren of Charles Derry, of Derry & Toms – and to Julia Gregson for her slinky 'house model' walk, as perfected for Debenham & Freebody, mid-Sixties.

Especial thanks to architect Benny O'Looney, champion of Peckham's past glories; to Judy Farraday and Gavin Henderson of John Lewis's comprehensive archive; and Sebastian Wormell of the great Harrods archive.

More generally, thanks to Glenys Jacques for her writing shed sanctuary, Katy Kelly for her writing retreats, Jacqueline Aldridge for literary references (who knew Barbara Pym shopped at Gamages?), Guy Arnold for vignettes from the Nineties shop floor, and Hattie Ellis for spotting pertinent snippets.

London's department stores were whole worlds, and they are mostly now vanished worlds. The communities they sustained are now disbanded, meeting only on Facebook groups with names like 'I Remember Pratts of Streatham'. Thank you for letting me gatecrash, and for sharing your memories.

Finally, gratitude is due to my husband Nick Glass for his many dogged and generous hours of research – and most of all, thanks to my editor and publisher Graham Coster for his idea, his forbearance over two years of pandemic, and his unflagging enthusiasm.

Further reading

For rich social history and context:
Adburgham, Alison, *Shops and Shopping 1800–1914: Where and in What Manner the Well-Dressed Englishwoman Bought her Clothes* (Barrie & Jenkins, 1989).
Cox, Pamela and Hobley, Annabel. *Shopgirls: The True Story of Life Behind the Counter* (Hutchinson, 2014).
Lancaster, Bill, *The Department Store: A Social History* (Leicester University Press, 2000).
Leach, William, *Land of Desire: Merchants, Power, and the Rise of a New American Culture* (Vintage, 1994).

The architectural story, illustrated:
Morrison, Kathryn, *English Shops & Shopping: An Architectural History* (Yale University Press, 2003).
Lloyd, Harriet, *Departing Stores: Emporia at Risk* (Save Britain's Heritage, 2022: available online).

For period detail:
Edwardian era: *Olivia's Shopping and How She Does It: A Prejudiced Guide to the London Shops*, 1906 – reprinted for the modern reader as 'The Essential Guide for the Edwardian woman-about-town, 1906'
1930s: Lovett, Vivien, *Kennards of Croydon: The Store That Entertained to Sell* (privately published in 2000, with access to the Kennards archive, available via second-hand booksellers).

Online archives
johnlewismemorystore.org.uk
housefraserarchive.ac.uk
historicengland.org.uk – for the Bedford LeMere picture collection

Blogs
thelondonwanderer.co.uk
Quirky, informative blog by Green Badge tourist guide Mark Pessell, bringing to life the stories of London's streets.
rbkclocalstudies.wordpress.com
The Library Time Machine: gently ruminative blogs and rare archive pictures by Dave Walker, Local Studies Librarian for the Royal Borough of Kensington and Chelsea.
eastend-memories.org
Charles Jenkins' lively blog on growing up in the East End in the Fifties and Sixties, including trips to department stores such as Gamages, J. R. Roberts and Wickhams.
cashrailway.co.uk
Niche, nerdy and wonderfully British website by Andrew Buxton on cash-carrying devices used in department stores. 'A labour of love', a treasure-trove of ephemera.

Contents

Lost Stores in Greater London

UXBRIDGE

Randalls

John Barnes

Jones
Brothers

Bearmans

Bodgers
Harrison Gibson

ILFORD

J R Roberts

Jeremiah
Rotherham

Wickhams

See map
opposite

The Royal
Arsenal
Co-operative
Society

Barbers

Jones &
Higgins

Holdrons

Chiesmans

Arding &
Hobbs

Quin & Axtens

Bon Marché

Pratts

CROYDON

Kennards

Allders

Grants

SUTTON

Shinners

Lost Stores in Central London

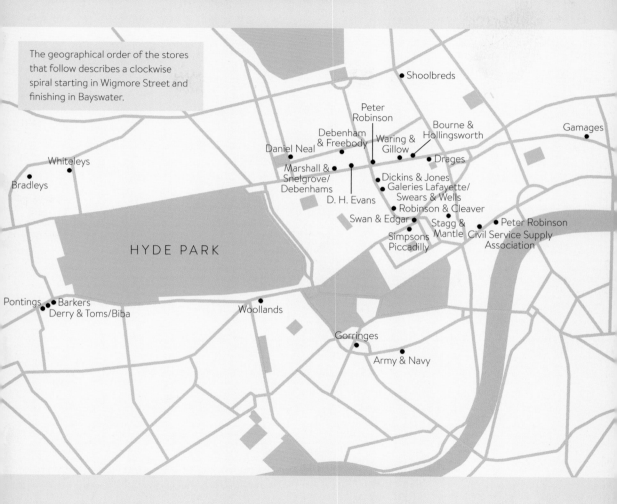

The geographical order of the stores that follow describes a clockwise spiral starting in Wigmore Street and finishing in Bayswater.

Shoolbreds

Gamages

Peter Robinson

Bourne & Hollingsworth

Debenham & Freebody

Waring & Gillow

Daniel Neal

Drages

Marshall & Snelgrove/ Debenhams

Dickins & Jones

D. H. Evans

Galeries Lafayette/ Swears & Wells

Robinson & Cleaver

Swan & Edgar

Peter Robinson

Stagg & Mantle

Civil Service Supply Association

Simpsons Piccadilly

Whiteleys

Bradleys

HYDE PARK

Pontings

Barkers

Derry & Toms/Biba

Woollands

Gorringes

Army & Navy

Introduction – A Journey into a Magic World

Who can forget the thrill of a first visit to a department store, especially at Christmas? Remember the sensory assault: displays to dazzle the eye, scents to enrapture, sweet treats to gorge on. You stepped onto the escalator and were transported up, higher and higher, as if on a magic carpet.

London's 'Halls of Temptation' were designed to seduce. They were the 'Great Emporia' of our Victorian and Edwardian ancestors, 'Cathedrals of Consumption,' 'as wonderful as any of the dream palaces of the Arabian Nights'. The first Christmas Grotto, dreamed up by J. R. Roberts of Stratford in 1888, put Santa in a darkened cavern lit by magic lanterns. Some 17,000

children visited. Thousands more marvelled at Blériot's monoplane, re-assembled inside Selfridges just 24 hours after its historic flight over the English Channel in 1909. And generations of men still remember standing for hours in Gamages, watching a Hornby train set shuttle around the shop floor.

By the early 1900s, London and its suburbs boasted over a hundred such department stores, often in bafflingly close proximity. Ilford had Bodgers *and* Harrison & Gibson; Peckham had Holdrons and Jones & Higgins. To modern eyes, the products and services on offer were extraordinary.

On Regent Street, the palatial Robinson & Cleaver would reduce the girth of your ankles while your beloved waited in a 'reading room for husbands'. Bon Marché of Brixton, with its fleet of liveried vans, guaranteed delivery to your London door in just one hour. Gamages sold alligators, Scouts' kits, magic tricks and motor accessories.

Today, little more than a handful survive. Of the rest, just the shells of buildings remain. Many have gone forever. But these are sites deeply connected with personal histories; sites where people gathered, loyally worked and celebrated life's milestones.

Let us enter one store – Woollands in Knightsbridge – on a morning in 1908, and draw back the curtain on a fitting room. 'Slithering around on her poor old knees', her mouth stuffed with pins, is a so-called 'fitter' known only as 'Number Ten'. She's measuring up young Sonia Keppell (daughter of King Edward VII's mistress, Alice) for a new riding habit. Half a century later, in another fitting

room, a 1950s schoolgirl named Sally Curtis is being fitted out by 'the amazing Mrs Boyce' at Daniel Neal in Portman Square, 'bangles a-jangling' as she works.

This book is a journey into a vanished world: 50 such worlds, each distinct in their way, and once much treasured. (It is a partial list only, for there were so many more: Gardiners of Stepney, Goslings of Richmond, Clements of Watford...) We will shadow the Edwardian 'shopping woman' into snooty Debenham & Freebody and down the 'Golden Mile' of Oxford Street, to the

fusty Army & Navy in Victoria, whose shop girls would eventually do the unthinkable and strike for more pay.

We will then follow her, and her descendants, into the Underground and off to suburbia, where the department store is even more deeply rooted. Mr Bearman of Leytonstone, Mr Allder of Croydon, Mr Chiesman of Lewisham – these are names that once supported armies of workers. Their stores and their stories have long since passed into folklore. Join us, as we step back in time and resurrect how so many of us used to shop.

DEBENHAM & FREEBODY

17–37 Wigmore Street, W1 • 1813–1975

The story of Debenhams is the quintessential British department store story: a tale of humble beginnings, ambitious expansion, grand apogee and painful decline. When Debenhams went into administration during the Coronavirus pandemic of 2020–21, it dealt a hammer blow to British retail history. All 124 stores closed with the loss of over 12,000 jobs. The brand's final collapse marked a watershed moment for the future of the department store – not just for the British high street, but for the capital. If London couldn't sustain even the flagship Debenhams on Oxford Street, what else would survive?

Britain's retail giant started in 1778 as an unassuming draper in Wigmore Street. William Clark was joined in 1813 by an aspiring 21-year-old from the Nottingham hosiery trade, hungry, ambitious, and with £500 to invest.

Fast-forward three decades, and William Debenham is presiding over a steadily expanding empire. He's brought in his son and his brother-in-law, Clement Freebody, creating 'Debenham, Son & Freebody'. He has opened branches in Cheltenham and Harrogate. 'Cavendish House' is now the grande dame of Wigmore Street, purveying luxurious silks, lace, haberdashery, millinery, mantles, lingerie, hosiery and every item essential to a Victorian lady in mourning (jet-black hairclips, fans, parasols, purses, gloves, hat bands). Soon he will be offering complete funeral services to his 'crème de la crème' clientele, drawn from aristocratic Cavendish Square.

Not for Debenhams the frantic obsession with stocking everything 'from a pin to an elephant', as with the more showman-like Whiteleys (the 'Universal Provider') or Harrods. At its heart, it remained a drapery and a fashion store with a thriving design, clothing production and wholesale arm. Debenham and

DEBENHAM & FREEBODY'S
NEW PREMISES.

THE MARBLE HALL.
From a painting by Byam Shaw.

DEBENHAM & FREEBODY'S PREMISES,
WIGMORE STREET, CAVENDISH SQUARE, LONDON, W.
From a painting by Mortimer Menpes.

Freebody is where the discerning Edwardian 'shopping lady' went to buy her entire wardrobe.

In 1906, 'Olivia', author of *A Prejudiced Guide to the London Shops*, singled it out for praise: a 'giant' among department stores, 'setting a standard of the best'. Not just, she noted, for its 'good and splendid furs', but 'for the wants of most people in less important things, and a special kind of black suede glove, which they sell at 1s.11 ½d, has made this shop a favourite with many quite economically-minded people.'

Debenham & Freebody's grand reconstruction on 17–37 Wigmore Street, almost opposite the Wigmore Hall, opened a year later, a Baroque revival confection clad in white Doulton Carrara tiles. Shoppers gasped in wonder at the new 'model gowns department' occupying a vast, square, top-lit space. Women now had a clubroom to repair to, with ceilings decorated in Arts & Crafts plasterwork by master craftsman Ernest Gimson; a uniquely safe public space where they could 'read their papers and magazines, telephone, write letters, or meet their friends'.

On the fourth floor a mahogany-panelled restaurant

A workroom at Debenham & Freebody, 1911. By now, women were the dominant workforce on the shop floor and behind the scenes.

was flanked by a spacious smoking room and a gentlemen's cloakroom. 'The most comfortable shop in the world' was, in itself, an entire world. Service was paramount. One staff notice warned that any employee found smoking Spanish cigars, getting shaved at a barber's shop or going to a dance would have their 'honesty and integrity' questioned. Yet there was also a staff education department, with thrice-weekly evening classes for young assistants.

All too soon, this fabulous rebuild was upstaged in 1909 by the opening of the flashier and modishly modern Selfridges, just round the corner on busy

Oxford Street. But Debenhams remained the pre-eminent empire builder, aggressively buying up rival names: Marshall & Snelgrove in 1919 (becoming the flagship Oxford Street

Debenhams on its 1979 rebuild), Harvey Nichols in 1920, Swan & Edgar and Drages in 1928, Woolland Bros in 1949 . . . By 1950 there were 110 stores across the UK.

While other branches of Debenhams courted the lower and middle classes during the leaner, inter-war years, its Wigmore Street headquarters retained an Edwardian air of opulence and exclusivity. 'Stately Debenhams' set the street's tone, noted the writer Harold Clun in 1950: 'the Rollses and Bentleys glide unctuously along, while the buses appear to be almost touching their caps with embarrassment. The dignified persona of the place, originally due to its being the shopping preserve of the Cavendish Square grandees is unmistakably dominant.'

Then came the Sixties, and unctuousness was suddenly out of step with the times. Joanna Lumley worked here as a 'house model' in 1966 on £8 a week, along with Julia Gregson, who remembers it as 'a terribly stuffy, big department store, quite expensive.' In the era of false eyelashes, Mary Quant shift dresses

and Vidal Sassoon haircuts, the store's house models – teenagers from Lucie Clayton's finishing school – were dressed up in tweeds and furs. 'There was this marvellous sort of slinky walk you had to do,' says Julia, 'when you slipped your coat off and dragged it behind you, swivelling, hands on hips, round the whole store.'

By this time, Debenham & Freebody's loyal clientele was increasingly elderly and eccentric. The store was falling out of fashion. And after 242 years of trading in fashion, that was something you could never afford to do. When Debenhams transferred its headquarters to the brutalist new building on Oxford Street, it was staking a claim on modernity.

DANIEL NEAL & SONS 3–7 Portman Square, W1 • 1937–1963

The name Daniel Neal acts as an instant trigger to many over the age of 50. This children's department store is where formative memories were made. The flagship Portland Square store in particular, with its dappled rocking horse, large doll's house and twisting Art Deco staircase, is indelibly fixed in the minds of generations.

Sally Curtis remembers being measured up for successive school blazers by 'the amazing Mrs Boyce, her arm of bangles a'jangling'. Clive Kandel remembers the downstairs shoe department, where young feet were X-rayed: 'Looking through that eye-shaped box at our green lit-up feet! Couldn't drag me away from it.' For Rosalie Osborne, it was the twice yearly treat of lunch with mother after the ritual of a school uniform fitting, aged four upwards.

If you hooked children in young, as department stores well knew, you had them for life. In 1953 Rosalie returned to Daniel Neal's with her mother on a special outing. Now aged 21, she had come to buy her first pram: a Marmet coach-built chassis in bottle green,

inside and out, with matching green cover. The pram, delivered to her Buckinghamshire home, was used for all three of her children. Visiting this store was a way of preserving a nostalgic connection not just with one's mother, but with one's own childhood.

The development of a children's consumer culture gathered pace in the mid-nineteenth century. Toys, clothes and furniture began to be marketed to celebrate and preserve children's unique, precious character. By the early twentieth century, parents were being urged by child psychologists and advertisers to equip separate playrooms with special furniture and stimulating toys. Clothes were no longer miniature versions of what their parents wore, but specially designed. Even the marketing language was different.

In 1919, Daniel Neals was advertising 'Baby's first real shoes' in the *Bystander*: 'Just a few pieces of cunningly fashioned leather, but the mother's heart weaves round them dreams of the golden path that the little feet are to tread. Phat Pheet are the "rightest" shoes for dimpled little feet – the best that money can buy.'

The original Daniel Neal started his business in 1837 as a bespoke shoemaker at 68–70 Edgware Road, but he died young, leaving his Scottish wife Elizabeth with five sons. Indignant at the way children's shoes were not made to fit chubby, growing feet, she developed a specialist children's shoe-fitting service in the 1870s. Her zeal inspired her sons. A new shop was opened at 120–126 Kensington High Street in 1911, focusing on children's footwear and clothing, followed by a complete, juvenile department store at 3–7 Portman Square in 1930.

Aligning themselves with smart private schools around Britain, Daniel Neal opened in Cheltenham in 1937, Bournemouth in 1947, Exeter in 1953 and Birmingham, 1960. They even infiltrated the private school system with a Daniel Neal chain of tuck shops.

Get them young, and you had them for life.

There was, however, one snag. Sales would boom before the start of a school year or new term, then understandably plummet. In 1963, the John Lewis Partnership purchased the chain and shut down the flagship store, absorbing the Portland Square stock into its Oxford Street store. The last two branches, Bournemouth and Cheltenham, were closed in 1977.

MARSHALL & SNELGROVE
334–348 Oxford Street, W1 · 1833–1975

One July morning in 1864, Lady Florence Paget and her fiancé Henry Chaplin entered Marshall & Snelgrove by the Oxford Street entrance then, momentarily, parted. He never saw her again. On the pretence of going to inspect the silk lingerie for her wedding trousseau, she ran through the store to the Vere Street exit, where she was met by the rakish

4th Marquis of Hastings. He whisked her off to St George's Hanover Square, and married her.

Smart society was scandalised, but none questioned the essentials of the story. It was a known fact that ladies like Lady Florence shopped at snooty Marshall & Snelgrove – and that this august department store, occupying an entire block, could swallow a person without trace. Behind its improvised façade was a rabbit warren: a higgledy-piggledy floor plan of departments speaking of rapid, piecemeal expansion ever since James Marshall opened a drapery store on Vere Street in 1833.

Even after its High Victorian facelift in 1878, Marshall & Snelgrove was notorious for what architects call a lack of 'flow'. But this was perhaps deliberate. By the 1890s a division between the Vere Street side, reserved for the store's exclusive clientele, and the Oxford Street side, which catered for 'less exalted customers', had been formalised. Enter from Vere Street, and you'd find yourself ushered by a fawning floor walker into a huge Mourning Room. Just a short bustle away was an equally spacious Silk Room, with smaller rooms for Ball and Fancy Dresses

'I worked as a trainee dressmaker at Marshall & Snelgrove in 1966, altering Model Gowns. The head of the department decided I was small enough to wear a stunning wedding dress that was never collected because the groom was killed in the war. The gown was Victorian and had pale pink silk ribbon threaded throughout.'

Lynne Bowles-Brown

and Trimmings. Push through the doors from Oxford Street, though, and you would access the more prosaic Haberdashery, Linens, Blankets and Carpets.

Although Marshall & Snelgrove claimed to be Oxford Street's first full-scale department store, the firm never branched out beyond high-class drapery and dressmaking. This was enough to create a great

retailing enterprise, with branches in Scarborough and Harrogate controlled from London. 'We know what we are and we mean to stick to it,' Yorkshireman John Marshall liked to put it.

By 1890 the store had just 25 departments (by 1906, Whiteley's had 159). It also had 800 employees, many accommodated like battery hens on the top three floors, two or four to a room. Did Marshall & Snelgrove fail to keep up with the times? 'Living in' became increasingly unpopular for workers, while the store's lack of architectural élan made it feel dowdy and outdated to the increasingly savvy Edwardian shopping woman – especially when the dazzling Selfridges opened a short walk away in 1909, its cavernous interior space lit up and exploited to the full.

The First World War compounded the store's struggles. The last remaining family member on the board, a great grandson of the founder, was killed in action in 1917. Two years later it was acquired by Debenhams as a prestigious status symbol, retaining the Marshall & Snelgrove name for its fashion cachet. The building was finally demolished and rebuilt between

Billowing Organdie for . . .
ASCOT'S PAGEANTRY

"MEADOW SWEET"
A Gown for Ascot cleverly combining a light air of sophistication with country simplicity, in white organdie over Taffeta, embroidered with field flowers, in red, yellow and blue, trimmed with a bunch of cornflowers at the waist - - - - - - 15½ Gns.

"MIGNONETTE"
An Ascot Gown in fine chiffon organdie over satin, in shades of blue, mauve and eau-de-nil, with mauve Taffeta sash, trimmed with panniers of lattice work in self material - - - - 15½ Gns.

THE HAT
A delightful Picture Hat from the Model Salon at Marshall, in burnt black hebe, with becoming deep tilt to the brim. The model has new effect floral trimming, and priced at - - - - - 5¼ Gns.

MODEL GOWNS—FIRST FLOOR

Marshall & Snelgrove
Tel. Mayfair 8400   *Debenhams Ltd*
VERE ST. & OXFORD ST. LONDON. W.I

1968 and 1979 to make way for Debenhams' flagship store – Oxford Street's 'ugly duckling' (according to the *Evening Standard*) in brutalist concrete.

A £40 million facelift in 2014 made a stab at reclaiming the store's lost glory: 180,000-worth of brushed aluminium tiles in a rippling, 'kinetic façade' by the artist Ned Khan. But now that the giant block sits empty, awaiting transformation into a retail and office scheme, this seems to smack of hubris. By the spring of 2022, workmen were already taking the tiles off again.

The Selfridges Effect

'From times immemorial woman has shopped,' proclaimed the *Daily Express* on 15 March 1909, 'but it is only since Monday that we have understood what the word really means.' The opening of Selfridges had ushered in a 'new era of shopping'.

Everything about Harry Gordon Selfridge's great

department store on Oxford Street was different – from the grandiose building, to the theatrical show windows, to the overt wooing of women. Happily, Selfridges is still a thriving and iconic store, acquired in 2021 by a Thai-Austrian partnership. But it belongs in this book because it was a game changer for the British department store.

As Mr Selfridge saw it, London's 'old-fashioned' retail meant it was ripe for the taking. He dismissed the big West End stores as 'an agglomeration of shops, formless and inefficient', with a 'subdued and disciplined' culture that actively discouraged fantasy

Costume Section.

or browsing. He agreed with steel magnate Andrew Carnegie, who'd visited in 1900 and recoiled. 'Just look at the jumble in the windows . . . so much stuff that you cannot take it all in. And when you go into a shop they treat you most indifferently. You are scowled at if you ask for goods out of the ordinary, and you are made to feel uncomfortable if you do not buy. These shop people drive away more people than they attract . . .

Shewing the location of SELFRIDGE'S with Mayfair in the foreground, Regent S.^t on the right, Piccadilly at bottom, Green Park at lower left hand, & Hyde Park & Marble Arch on left of Print.

What London wants is a good shaking up.'

Selfridge was the man to do it. Everything about his great store would be different. The building rose at speed from a double-depth basement, reinforced with immense steel girders and concrete foundations. His advertisements (a media blitz costing £36,000) spoke explicitly to women. Shopping at Selfridges would be

THE HANGING GARDENS OF LONDON. SELFRIDGES WATER GARDENS. LOOKING WEST

'A Pleasure – A Pastime – A Recreation . . . something more than merely shopping'. Browsing was encouraged; no need to buy! Here you would find spectacle, theatre, sociability, a safe haven. Here was a complete day out, 'a social centre, not a shop'. There was even a Silence Room where shoppers could take 'a rest cure from the whirl of bargains and build up energy'.

The working culture would also be different. Selfridge treated his staff exceptionally well, personally visiting every department daily. He introduced the term 'shop assistant', and actively crusaded against the term 'shop girl', which he believed to be 'an epitaph almost

of disrespect'. He changed the way people in Britain shopped.

There was, inevitably, great resentment at this American entrepreneur, but most retailers felt obliged to adopt his successful strategies or go under. Soon, all stores were being referred to as 'pleasure centres'. They increased their advertising, spruced up their windows, rebuilt and redesigned their gloomy interiors. Harrods made sure its sixtieth anniversary, celebrated in 1909, was memorably lavish. Not to be outdone, Whiteleys built an entirely new store and marked its opening in 1911 with swagger.

The ripple effect of Selfridges was both immediate and long lasting. 'Every West End firm vied with one another to dazzle and entertain its customers,' reported the *Daily Express* a day after the store's grand opening. 'Oxford Street, Regent Street, and Brompton Road were crowded with eager shoppers. Never before has it been possible for the twentieth-century woman to indulge in such an orgy of shopping.'

D. H. EVANS 318 Oxford Street, W1 · 1878–2001

It was the perfect promotional opportunity. The 1937 coronation of King George VI coincided with the unveiling of the triumphantly modernist D. H. Evans. And since the six-mile processional route would pass before the new-look store (now offering an paralleled view from its fifth-floor restaurant, higher than anything else on Oxford Street), it seemed entirely natural to shout out about it.

D. H. Evans' commemorative Coronation brochure was a brilliant piece of self-publicity: lavishly illustrated, seductively worded, its aerial cover shot incontestable proof of the store's superior size. The old, two-building, Edwardian incarnation of D. H. Evans was swiftly forgotten. There was now just one giant London department store of note – and it wasn't Selfridges.

'London's Most Modern Shop' was a statement building: steel frame, concrete floors, a façade of Portland stone above pale grey granite. Behind this 'German Art-Deco' design was a Scot: Louis David Blanc, Harrods' in-house architect. Recent relaxation of height restrictions meant the new building could rise to a dizzying 100 feet. Not only did this give it tremendous street presence, it also produced one of London's most exciting spaces.

The escalator hall was the store's focal point,

D. H. Evans used some of the most innovative illustrators of the day, such as Hungarian émigré Arpad Elfer for the 1950s 'Fashion Wise' London Underground posters, and Habitat designer Juliet Glynn Smith to evoke psychedelic Swinging London in the 1960s.

Artist Maggi Giles worked in the store's Sales Promotion office from the age of 17 to 20, dressing the wall displays while fending off 'a mass of frenzied customers' who

would 'bear down purposefully on her', mistaking her for a sales assistant. Maggi's 1958 'New Year's Resolutions' cartoon was distributed in house to staff amusement. 'I will endeavour to be pleasant and helpful under ALL circumstances,' vows the shop assistant, as a spoilt madam returns a crumpled outfit.

a glamorous place to be seen as well as to see. Trippers flocked for the thrill of this hall alone – not only the criss-crossing escalators serving five floors, but the

high-speed elevators, taking you straight to the top. When young Margaret Pinsent was taken on a day trip to London from Oxford in 1940, she remembered 'not

An impression of the Escalator and Lift Hall

the bombs, but the elevators in D. H. Evans'.

It was a highly sensory, opulent environment. The walls and pillars were of 'delicate beige-pink' Travertine marble, the floors of polished cork, producing a 'soft, brown glow' (to quote the brochure). The fibrous plaster ceiling was in a 'modernistic design', the sheen

of metalwork on stairs, escalators and lifts was achieved through 'silver and copper bronze surfaces, satin finished'.

It was the place to go to be pampered. Half the fourth floor was devoted to hairdressing and beauty salons with 'an all-British staff'. Cubicles boasted 'padded comfort chairs, spring rests for the feet, a telephone, and sterilising cabinets.' Nine 'sound-proof' beauty rooms used products prepared in D. H. Evans' own laboratories. There were on-site workshops 'for the production of postiche' (hair pieces).

While mothers indulged in Thirties beauty culture, their children could be left in 'Peter Pan's Playground' – a fantasy environment of tree houses, ornamental ponds and fountains. The whole store was, in effect, an adult fantasy environment, in imitation of the great

American department stores. By 1937, the connection to D. H. Evans' Welsh Baptist origins had been comprehensively sundered.

Dan Harries Evans was a draper's apprentice from South Wales who moved to London in 1877, acquiring a shop on Westminster Bridge Road with his dressmaker wife. The business moved to Oxford Street in 1879,

gradually taking over adjoining buildings, until – by 1894 – D. H. Evans was a limited company employing some 400 staff. A five-floor, Edwardian rebuild in Italian marble followed in 1910, in use for just 25 years. When D. H. Evans merged with Harrods in 1928 (the two stores having long shared management staff), Harrods' chairman Sir Woodman Burbidge schemed to consolidate this two-site Oxford Street department store with one, impressive block. 'London's Most Modern Shop' was the result.

Alas, that glowing cork floor, the rose-pink marble walls and the softly gleaming metalwork didn't survive

The 1937 D. H. Evans building rose to a dizzying height and heft, topped only by the modernist John Lewis in 1960.

the purging refurbishments of 1982, 1985 and 1999 under the ownership of House of Fraser (which acquired the Harrods group in 1954). In 2001 the name D. H. Evans disappeared from Oxford Street for good. Name changes were 'not a big deal for shoppers', claimed CEO John Coleman, who rebranded the store 'House of Fraser': there was, he said, little loyalty attached to the name D. H. Evans. Customers and shop workers felt otherwise. When the iconic store shut in January 2022, there was much nostalgia for its former incarnation.

DICKINS & JONES
224–244 Regent Street, W1 • 1835–2006

One afternoon in 1859, the journalist and author George Augustus Sala sallied down Regent Street, recording his impressions for a book. Sala was drawn irresistibly to the plate glass windows of the 'magnificent linen drapery establishments' that lined the fashionable street, where young men and women assistants were 'accomplishing the difficult and mysterious feat known as "dressing" the shop window'.

Their art dazzled him. 'By their nimble and practised hands, the richly piled velvet mantles are displayed, the moiré and glace silks arranged in artful folds, the laces and gauzes, the innumerable whim-whams and fribble-frabble of fashion elaborately shown'.

Dickins & Jones occupied a prime position at the top of Regent Street, its long windows stretching across three building blocks. The department store's famous 'white sales' consisted of ingenious displays, in which hundreds of snowy fabrics and clothes were twisted, folded and heaped up to create extraordinary window

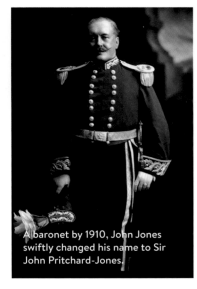

A baronet by 1910, John Jones swiftly changed his name to Sir John Pritchard-Jones.

tableaux. On 22 January 1901, the day before the Winter White Sale's grand unveiling, Queen Victoria died. As one assistant remembered it, 'by next morning, everything was turned black. It was one of the biggest transformations in the trade.'

This *grande dame* of department stores can trace its roots back to 1790, and a drapery partnership between Thomas Dickins and William Smith, moving from Oxford

Five years after Jones's death, a grand new building opened in 1922. Now Harrods owned the business.

to Regent Street in 1835. When Queen Victoria began shopping here, the store's reputation was sealed. It then took a Welsh farmer's son to shake things up and take the store into the twentieth century. Joining in 1872, John Jones was successively promoted to buyer, manager, director, chairman of the board and finally to partner, when the store's name was changed to Dickins & Jones.

Jones – by now sporting a horizontal, waxed moustache and a white bow tie – was a ball of energy. He dabbled in other businesses; he campaigned to promote workers' welfare; he promoted profit-sharing schemes for his employees. In the 1900s he engineered a spate of acquisitions: silk mercers Lewis & Allenby and George Hitchcock; baby linen retailers Balls & Flint; Redmayne the high-class tailors. By the 1910s the

Dickins family wanted out, and Harrods Stores Ltd was invited by Jones to take a controlling interest. Customers knew little of this. The store was sought out for its ladies' fashions, and for a certain old-fashioned attention to detail that percolated right through to the 1895 tea room. 'Do you ever happen to recollect the dark, sad days when you had not heard of the Dickins and Jones Tea-room?' asks Olivia, in her 'Prejudiced Guide' to the London shops, 1906. 'I can never forget their shining coffee kettles, nor the quality of their tea. You may buy it by the pound after you have tried it. I generally do, after a cup there.'

A new store designed by Sir Henry Tanner rose slowly over the 1920s and 30s, boasting an even lovelier tea room, a restaurant and a library. Tanner drew inspiration from multiple influences – Egyptian, Roman and French. *Country Life*'s critic gleefully savaged the result. 'With its ornate details, its black balconies and attics above attics', the new Dickins & Jones was like 'the finale of some old-fashioned music comedy'.

Was it old-fashioned? During the 1950s, the store was a destination for elegant women's fashion. It employed some 1,000 staff. When Harrods was bought by House of Fraser in 1959, both Harrods and Dickins & Jones continued to trade under their existing names. It was a sudden, shocking, twenty-first-century rent rise – from £250,000 to £4.5 million per annum – that forced House of Fraser to close the historic department store in 2006.

Looking ahead

in Regent Street

DICKINS AND JONES

Post-war glamour came to Dickins & Jones with the hiring of advertising agency Colman Prentice & Varley (CPV). Under its innovative art director Arpad Elfer, brands such as Fortnum & Mason, D. H. Evans, Elizabeth Arden, Yardley and Jaeger were getting modern facelifts in the hands of bold illustrators. The 'lady in the rose' was conceived for Dickins & Jones in 1954 by the fashion artist René Gruau (responsible for Dior's 'New Look'), creating the iconic logo still associated with the store.

GALERIES LAFAYETTE · 186–196 Regent Street, W1 · 1920–1972

One of the Parisian *grand magasins* swept into town in 1920. '"Dazzle" is to be the keynote of the new business,' the French manager George Planques told the *Daily Express*, promising 'midnight displays' of lingerie, and new *modes* from Paris every night. 'We intend to bring Paris to London . . . with the most chic gowns the French capital can turn out. An aeroplane

will bring new fashions over to us every day.' The famous Lafayette wax models would also be flown over, complete with French 'scenery'. A photograph taken at night in 1929 shows a ghostly scene of mannequins framed by the store's Art Deco frontage, glowing in the dark.

The original Galeries Lafayette on Paris's Boulevard Haussmann was conceived as a 'luxury bazaar', a sumptuous Art Deco palace to consumerism with its glittering, stained-glass cupola. After years of preparation, it grandly opened in 1912 with the aim of

'awakening all envies, desires, possibilities'. Now this ambition extended to London.

The Regent Street store was on a smaller scale, but with a substantial shop front along numbers 186–196 (leasing space from Swears & Wells, and an adjacent furriers, Victory & Co). In 1923 the *Westminster Gazette* was agog at the window displays of this

'truly Parisian house' – 'a pageant of beautiful women,' dressed by expert French hands. The models were set in a fashionable tableau – on a cruise ship, perhaps, or in a salon drinking a *digestif*.

The human-haired, glass-eyed, porcelain-toothed, wax mannequins of Pierre Imans were famous for their realism. Here were matinee idols with cleft jaws and disdainfully curling lips; open-faced youths with eyes full of emotion; chuckling uncles with florid cheeks and bushy eyebrows. His women came in all shapes and sizes – flat chests, wide hips, middle-aged faces. They reflected (way before their time) the diverse body shapes of women: those potential customers gazing at the clothes on show through large, steel-framed, plate glass windows.

The Dutch-born Imans described himself not as a wax modeller but a 'sculptor' – and Londoners clustered outside the windows of the Galeries Lafayette on Regent Street to stare at the uncannily life-like results. These were not mannequins but *créations artistiques*, as he put it, 'great masterpieces of modern sculpture'.

The department store managed to keep its youthful French pizazz into the Sixties, but couldn't compete with London's new range of boutiques. It closed in 1972, and in 1981 the site was taken over by Hamley's toy store.

SWEARS & WELLS 190–196 Regent Street, W1; 374 Oxford Street, W1 • 1816–1970

This is where Alice Keppell, mistress to King Edward VII, ritually took her daughters to be fitted up for their riding habits. Sonia remembers 'sitting erect on the girth section of a wooden horse' in the correct riding posture, and leaving equipped with 'bowler-hats, covert coats and thong-less whips. Violet, a riding-habit' (Violet was the eldest); 'me, some breeches.' Swears & Wells styled itself 'The First establishment in

the World' for children's clothing. The so-called 'Lilliputian Warehouse' was established at 192 Regent St in 1816 by Frederick Swears and Thomas William Wells, with the aim of fitting out boys and 'young ladies' for a closely prescribed life in the upper social strata. Suits for schoolboys were 'drafted by the best cutters, upon lines approved by the headmasters of the great public schools of England.'

The store was patronised by the Royals, the Empress of Russia, the Empress of Germany, the King of Spain . . . 'not excluding the leaders of New York and Boston society' (as a *Handbook to the Season* noted in 1892). There was an undeniable snob value to shopping here, but the label's reputation for high quality was deserved. Mothers swore by 'Swears'. For Jane Ellen Panton, writing in the *Ladies Pictorial* in 1888, there

was only one make of jacket and trouser that would 'defy the rough usage' of her three boys. True, the cost was 'rather awful to contemplate', but the items 'undoubtedly outwear three suits of anyone else's.'

The other great specialism of Swears & Wells was fur. The windows of the 1920s Art Deco rebuild show

mannequin flappers in slim coats with lavish collars and cuffs in fox, ermine, beaver and mink. By 1935, the firm claimed to be the largest furrier in the world, operating from Regent Street, a store at 374 Oxford Street, and several other regional branches. At the outbreak of World War II, when fur prices 'doubled overnight', they offered 'Pre-war prices while stocks last.'

Swears & Wells was the obvious choice to supply furs to a 1960 British film comedy, *Make Mine Mink*, starring Terry-Thomas and Hattie Jacques. But the fur trade was now increasingly ostracised, and the company (which had grown to 16 regional branches) couldn't recover. At the time of their closing-down sale at 374 Oxford Street, in 1970, it was offering '£36,000 worth of glorious furs, half price or less'.

From Bedbugs to Bible Classes

The Living Hell of 'Living-In'

In 1891, some half a million shop assistants 'lived-in', trapped in a system that paid partly in cash, partly with board and lodging. Some six to twenty young men or women might share a room in cramped and unsanitary conditions, expected to turn up for work looking spotless in their black silk dresses and buttoned

Whiteleys shop assistants campaigning against the loathed 'living-in' system, 1901.

waistcoats. Money would be deducted from their wages for 'extras' such as baths (one pint of hot water per person per week), while fines were dished out for sins such as 'untidiness', 'leaving the gaslight on', or 'entertaining visitors', especially of the opposite sex. 'Living-in' was said to discourage immorality – yet shopgirls were routinely harassed, often by men trying to pay late-night visits. If apprehended, they would claim to have 'thought it a brothel'.

By the late nineteenth century, the grander department stores couldn't risk being called out for bedbugs or rising damp in their dormitories. William Whiteley was one who spent lavishly to house his workers nearby and in relative comfort. Bedrooms were shared by up to three girls and furnished with feather beds, a washstand and a chest of drawers.

From the Edwardian era onwards, large stores began (with much publicity) to announce the 'setting free' of their workforce. Those that clung on to the system took staff accommodation to new heights: nestled in

How Harrods Wooed its Workers

By 1890, Harrods of Knightsbridge employed an incredible 5,000 staff. But the store's brusque and paternalistic management style was unpopular and outdated – until Richard Burbidge was hired from Whiteleys to become General Manager. Burbidge was a progressive. He abolished fines, reduced working hours and held Sunday Bible classes at his home. South of the river in Barnes he established the Harrodian Club for evening activities, and set up the Harrodian Amateur Athletic Association.

Driving all this was the opening of Selfridges and its more enlightened management culture. Burbidge's son Woodman took things further, as general manager between 1911 and 1935, starting the *Harrodian Gazette* and evening classes in anything from handwriting to Spanish. Other department stores were by now doing the same, offering

many grand rooflines were dormitories with rows of small, ornate windows. The risk of fire was, however, a constant hazard. Reports of staff burning to death (as happened at Barkers of Kensington in 1912, when five shopgirls died in the eaves) did not make for good publicity.

Staff training at Harrods, 1920. Classrooms were strictly segregated.

Bourne & Hollingsworth's staff swimming pool.

swimming pools and libraries, hiking clubs and choirs, inter-store football matches and amateur dramatics.

At its best, working for a big store was akin to joining a family.

Tired Slaves or Bright Sparks?

In the *Daily News*, in January 1912, the writer G. K. Chesterton lashed out at 'The Big Shop' – those 'awful interminable emporia . . . how I always imagine hell, even in my sleep'. Female shop assistants were, he wrote, 'the tired slaves of a colourless system'. Outraged, Selfridges' female shop assistants hit back in a letter with 180 signatories. They argued that quite the opposite was the case. 'We are proud to have in our ranks some of the brightest intelligences associated with commerce. We look upon ourselves as members of a "Business Republic" . . . where free speech, free thought, and general initiative is expected to be shown on all occasions.' These women were constantly educating themselves, this Easter visiting 'as a business refresher, the largest department stores and speciality houses of Paris'.

ROBINSON & CLEAVER

156–170 Regent Street, W1 • 1894–1984

What must it have felt like, walking into one of those 'gigantic mercantile emporia' in the golden age of the department store? Newspaper reports on the palatial 1904 rebuild of Irish linen merchants Robinson & Cleaver give some idea of the dazzle, the spectacle, the seduction and sheer ambition of this confident era.

'Metropolitan shops have long been the objects of unfavourable criticism by our Parisian neighbours,' wrote the *Daily News* reporter. 'Now Londoners will have one shop, at least, which will compare favourably

John Cleaver (left) and Edward Robinson

with any to be seen in the French capital.' The new store boasted a 'magnificent' marble staircase with alabaster balustrades and hand rail, flanked by life-size marble statues of Erin (goddess of Ireland) and Britannia. The reporter walked, breathlessly, up those stairs, and found himself facing three, 'immense' stained glass windows, rising 27 feet high.

The *Pall Mall Gazette* proclaimed Robinson and Cleaver's 'new saloons of fashion', spread over eight splendid floors, 'superb'. Here was 'everything an

Edwardian lady could want' – 'real lace and linen, fancy openwork tea cloths and table centres, wonderful bedspreads, dreams of beauty in the silk and dress department, colienne and chiffon in delicate tints . . .'

In 2015, Historic England was given a rare album comprising 11 large, sepia-toned prints of the Robinson & Cleaver department store on Regent Street, taken in about 1910 by an unknown photographer. Almost all are of the interior with its proudly displayed merchandise, giving us a unique chance to enter a great Edwardian emporium – 'one of the most palatial establishments in London', thought the *Pall Mall Gazette* in 1904. Note the marble columns, wrought iron lift and gleaming electric lights.

He agreed with the others: this was indeed 'the most palatial establishment in London'.

Yet this building was just a satellite, an Irish toehold on London's premier street. 'From the Land of Lace and Linen' went the tagline on Robinson & Cleaver's advertisements. 'American visitors are invited to inspect our very extensive stocks of Irish hand-made goods'– this from the *Cunard Daily Bulletin* aboard RMS *Etruria*. Everyone knew that American tourists made straight for Regent Street.

Edward Robinson and John Cleaver set up business together in Belfast in 1870, providing good quality local goods at reasonable prices. The city soon grew into one of the major manufacturing centres of the British Empire, and business boomed, as the highest class of Irish fabrics – double damask, table linen, Irish embroideries, lace – was dispatched the length and breadth of the Empire. Over one-third of all parcels posted in Belfast in 1887 were sent from the Royal Irish Linen Warehouse, as Robinson & Cleaver was known.

That year, an enormous, neo-classical edifice rose on the corner of Donegall Place and Donegall Square, designed by Young and MacKenzie. The new Belfast store was sumptuous, inside and out. It had six storeys, a clock tower, ogee copper domes and a flock of Donatello cherubs carved by Harry Helms of Exeter. Fifty stone heads of the firm's patrons peered down from on high, including Queen Victoria, the Emperor and Empress of Germany, Lady Dufferin (Vicerene of India) and General Washington. Inside was . . . a magnificent, curving marble staircase, flanked by Erin and Britannia.

The Edwardian London store wasn't an exact replica, but it contained many elements of the Robinson & Cleaver formula. Architects Crickmay & Sons gave it the requisite copper domes, ornate balustrades and its own seated lions, silhouetted against the skyline. Inside was that staircase, eight fabulous floors of fashion, and Lamson Pneumatic Tubing to save delays at cash desks (there were just two other shops with this in 1904: the Bon Marché, and Roberts of Stratford).

Once so thoroughly modern, though, Robinson & Cleaver failed to keep pace. By the Sixties, both the Regent Street and Belfast stores were regarded as fussy and old-fashioned. The business was finally closed in 1984. The imposing corner entrance at 156 Regent Street is now a branch of the Spanish clothing chain Massimo Dutti.

PETER ROBINSON

214–236 Oxford Street, W1 • 1833-1974   65 Strand, WC2 • 1958-1974

Peter Robinson dealt with the upper classes, and it dealt with death. A macabre carriage fitted with black horses stood ready at all times outside the Victorian store, topped with two coachmen in black, complete with crape hat, arm bands and whips with crape bows. Two lady fitters, also dressed in black, sat inside the carriage clutching pattern and mourning

Victorians queue outside 'Black Peter's', the Court and Family Mourning Warehouse.

etiquette books. The call to visit a house newly plunged into mourning could, and did, come hourly. Grief was big business.

When Prince Albert died aged 42 just before Christmas in 1861, the British Empire was plunged into formal mourning. Regent Street was the London centre for mourning wear, and Peter Robinson was quick to secure a warehouse here alongside his Oxford Circus island site (founded as a haberdashery in 1833). It became known as Black Peter Robinson, a place where the design, construction and embellishment of dresses

changed 'well nigh every week'.

Scrupulous attention to detail endeared Peter Robinson to the upper classes. This was a family draper that knew about place, social and material. Carriages would draw up outside the Oxford Circus entrance and, as one staff member put it, 'the duchesses would step out.' A liveried page boy in white gloves would deliver them to an impressive figure in a mourning coat at the store entrance, who in turn would summon an unctuous shopwalker to escort customers to the counter required, pulling out a chair while they were shown the latest consignment of fine Brussels lace. The whole pantomime would be performed in reverse, back into the waiting carriage.

That same staff member lamented the fall in standards brought about by interlopers. 'Oxford Street was a superior shopping street until Bourne & Hollingsworth and then Selfridges brought the general trade!' (in 1902 and 1909). When Harry Gordon Selfridge visited London in 1890, he regarded Peter Robinson as one of nine London department stores that were 'all soundly established', but 'run by

A second Peter Robinson, opened in the Strand in 1958, lays claim to be one of our shortest lived department stores. It was the first in Britain to make use of large-scale bronze classing, and contained a starkly modern interior. But in less than two decades the chain was no more, and by 1996 this striking brutalist building – an early work of Denys Lasdun (later of National Theatre fame) – had been demolished.

accountants'. He also took issue with the store's ethos, that it was 'better to do an exclusive trade than a big trade'.

And yet 'Olivia', in her anonymous 1906 shopping guide, applauds Peter Robinson for the very pedantry that so irritated Mr Selfridge – 'the latent stability of the Victorian era', as she puts it. The staff simply knew what they were doing. 'At Peter Robinson's are the experts. These are trained people, who discriminate scientifically between cotton and wool, and tell you the truth about it – not languid persons of many manners and no knowledge, who will swear cotton is silk to have done with you. If Peter Robinson's say things will wear well, they generally do.'

Few shoppers would have been aware that those who served them lived in-house, in conditions described as 'a blend of semi-monastic institution and the fairly strict boarding school'. The store was one of the last to make the transition to staff 'living out', only after its grand new premises opened on the redeveloped Oxford Circus in 1912 (including a 700-seat restaurant on the top floor, complete with vibrant operatic murals).

Peter Robinson was acquired in 1946 by Burton's, which retained the name, creating a 39-store chain. Burton also created a love child that would, in time, eclipse its conservative parent. Peter Robinson's Topshop opened in the Oxford Circus store basement in 1965. By 1974, there was only one winner.

For many years the flagship of Sir Philip Green's Arcadia empire, the former restaurant with its spectacular arched ceiling repurposed as the company's accounts department, Topshop closed its doors in 2021. The building has now been acquired by IKEA for its first West End store.

A New Kind of Freedom

The Girling of Shopwork

In 1900, a quarter of a million women worked in shops. By the mid-1960s, the number was over a million, nearly one-fifth of the country's female workforce. Department stores were the first institutions that opened the door of middle and high management to women, creating perhaps the first career structure

Gendered space: the millinery department at Morgan Squire of Leicester, 1900.

with genuine prospects of promotion. Today, women are such familiar figures behind the till and the counter and in the boardrooms of retail chains that it's hard to imagine shop life without them. But until the 1860s, when the first wave of 'shop girls' began to break into retail, British shops were dominated by men.

Yet women, it was discovered, came cheap. A shop girl in the 1870s might receive around £25 a year, while her male counterpart would take home £40. Previous concerns about respectability and gentility, about women not being physically strong enough or professional enough to work on the shop floor,

FOR THE SHOP GIRL.

VEN-YUSA
Remedies Jaded Looks.

evaporated as soon as the monetary benefits became clear. And so shopkeepers became the unlikely allies of the early feminists.

Shop work offered young women financial independence, a new kind of freedom, and the chance to better themselves. The female customers preferred them. Only the female shop assistant could 'fathom the agony of despair as to the arrangement of colours, the alternative trimmings, the duration of a fashion and the depths of a woman's purse', wrote society hostess and journalist Lady Jeune in 1895.

By the early twentieth century, women were in the majority. The 'girling' of shopwork had created, in the words of one American department store owner, 'an Adamless Eden.'

'An Adamless Eden'

The department store became the first public place where women could meet without any escort. The buildings were increasingly luxurious: domed roofs, marbled walls, Eastern carpets and plush armchairs. Orchestras played in the restaurants; fashion shows were held in the foyers. There were tea rooms, writing rooms, powder rooms, hair salons – even crèches. Most

A snatched rest for shop assistants in 'Room Six' at Harrods, 1920.

importantly, there were lavatories.

Harry Gordon Selfridge's quietly revolutionary move in 1909 was to introduce a ladies' lavatory, the first in a London department store. He saw – as other owners had not – that women might want to stay in town all day, without having to use a public convenience. In this small but significant way, he promoted women's emancipation. 'I came along just at the time when women wanted to step out on their own,' he later said.

'A Mass of Femininity'

'Buying and selling, serving and being served – women. On every floor, in every aisle, at every counter, women . . . Behind most of the counters on all the floors . . . women. At every cashier's desk, at the wrapper's desks, running back and forth with parcels and change, short-skirted women. Filling the aisles, passing and re-passing, a constantly arriving and departing throng of shoppers, women. Simply a moving, seeking, hurrying, mass of femininity, in the midst of which the occasional man shopper, man clerk, and man supervisor, looks lost and out of place.'

Hampton's Magazine, 1910

WARING & GILLOW   164–182 Oxford Street, W1 · 1903–1980

In June 1906, a red-and-white palazzo was unveiled on the eastern half of Oxford Street. It drew its inspiration from the elaborate red-brick façade of Hampton Court Palace, boasted a soaring rotunda of 85 by 54 feet, and was designed by the architect later pulled in to finesse Selfridges (which opened the following year).

Waring & Gillow was a dazzling triumph for architect R. Frank Atkinson. But the real genius behind this bold and innovative new store was the businessman who appointed him. Samuel James Waring – all but forgotten today – was highly influential to the development of the British department store. Waring pushed Britain's taste boundaries, bringing the 'modern' into our homes. He introduced the concept of interior design to the masses, hand-picking an extraordinary team to deliver it. He coaxed his friend Harry Gordon Selfridge into business (creating 'Selfridge & Waring' in 1906), negotiating permissions and lending him his architect. Both men were disruptors to the staid status quo.

Waring & Gillow didn't do fashion, but fixtures and fittings. What began in 1903 as a formal merger between two highly respected collaborators – Warings of Liverpool and Gillows of Lancaster – went on to become furnishers and decorators to King George V. They fitted out royal yachts and luxury ocean liners, such as the ill-fated *Lusitania* (1906) and the *Queen Mary* (1936). They furnished prestigious hotels and West End theatres – the Carlton, Ritz and Waldorf, the Lyceum and the Savoy.

The new department store had a rather different goal. 'Furniture for the Million and the Millionaire', went a 1907 advertisement in the *Graphic*.

Waring wanted to re-educate the masses. Interior design should be for all. Taste could be learned, formed, pushed in new directions. He conceived the idea of 'Five Model Houses', not unlike today's IKEA showrooms, furnished for five different budgets: £100, £200, £300, £500 or £750. In 1922, Lloyd George made him a peer for being a 'pioneer of decorative art in furnishing', as well as a generous philanthropist. Six years later, excited by the modern designs coming out of Europe, Lord Waring played his masterstroke. He appointed the Russian émigré architect and designer Serge Chermayeff (pictured; distinguished today as co-designer of the Art Deco De La Warr Pavilion in Bexhill-on-Sea) as director of an experimental Modern Art Department within the Oxford Street department store.

An international design team was assembled – French, Italian, Hungarian, one Brit, and just one woman (French). The result was a landmark show that ran for three months in 1928, featuring 68 fully decorated and furnished rooms on the store's fourth and fifth floors. Thousands visited 'Modern

Art in French and English Furniture and Decoration'. The vibe was *moderne*: smooth cuboid lines, discordant colour schemes, jazzy French textiles. Materials included rubber, plate glass, tubular steel and plywood. It was a watershed moment for a London department store, elevating consumer goods to the status of artefacts.

If you want a Cottage furnished, or a House, or a Palace –

If you want a single article of furniture or house equipment –

If you want china, glass, ironmongery, brushes, plated or silver goods, cutlery, clocks, bronzes, trunks, electrical fittings, upholsteries, pianos, fancy goods, books, stationery, bed and table linen or carpets –

The Only Place is Waring's New Galleries.

In 1930 the profligate Lord Waring was forced to resign as chairman; the Modern Art Department folded a year later. Both were highly influential in their time. And although the name Waring & Gillow has long disappeared from Oxford Street (it merged with Maples in 1980, which in turn was swallowed by Allied, that went into receivership in 1997), the name is still highly coveted in the antiques world today. Just take a look on eBay.

Today the building is home to branches of fashion chains H&M and Uniqlo.

BOURNE & HOLLINGSWORTH · 116–118 Oxford Street, W1 · 1902–1983

It was a favourite place to meet: beneath the Art Deco clock in the centre of Bourne and Hollingsworth. For a certain sort of respectable, conservative Home Counties woman, this was the destination on a day up to town: the store where the staff stopped just short

BOURNE & HOLLINGSWORTH LTD., OXFORD STREET. W. 1

of serving you a sherry (as *The Times* put it). Suave and soothing, unchanging and unchallenging, Bourne & Hollingsworth knew its niche and never strove to be 'with it', deliberately targeting an 'ordinary' middle-class clientele, making a virtue of its familiarity, homeliness and safety. This was an overtly family firm – but that

strength was, in the end, its downfall.

Drapers Walter William Bourne and Howard Hollingsworth set up business together in Westbourne Grove in 1894. Bourne married Hollingsworth's sister Clara; the business flourished; they moved to the eastern, less fashionable end of Oxford Street in 1902 and established a solid, un-showy reputation. The family dynasty grew. William Bourne had seven children; their descendants included 19 first cousins. By 1977 some 73 family members were shareholders, making it near impossible to make bold decisions in the store's best interest.

Bourne and Hollingsworth's timid Twenties rebuild was a typically cautious company decision. Mindful that it would need to see the store through many decades, Stafford Bourne chose with prudence, avoiding fashionable modern architects in favour of a close

family friend and neighbour.

The muted Art Deco building already felt slightly out of date when unveiled in 1925, at precisely the time when the best of London's retail architecture was becoming highly experimental, drawing on the talents of some of the best modern architects such as Joseph Emberton (creator of Simpson's). But playing it safe had its positives. This was a safe place to work, highly paternalistic. Staff were superbly well looked after.

Howard Hollingsworth's memories of his own

apprenticeship – poor food and accommodation in a rat-infested basement – made him a sympathetic employer. The firm was among the first to employ a large number of women assistants, housing them in socially progressive, bespoke hostels in Store and Gower Streets, Bloomsbury – the latter boasting a swimming pool (see pages 34-35), ballroom and library. In return, the store was renowned for its high standards of staff discipline, appearance and courtesy.

In 1959 the business expanded, becoming Southampton's 'classiest shop in town' (as nostalgic customers remember), with a 'wonderful sweeping staircase with shiny brass hand rail.' It lasted just 20 years. When old-fashioned Bourne & Hollingsworth was bought up in 1978 by the East End garment manufacturer Raybeck, its workforce was of prime concern to the family. None survived. Within five years the department store was filled with concessions such as W.H. Smith and Allied Carpets, taken downmarket, then closed. By then, it was no longer the 'gracious institution' mourned by *The Times*. Reports in 1984 of an attempt to sell the famous Art Deco clock, fondly regarded as a symbol of the store, suggest a failure to understand Bourne & Hollingsworth's special status in the public imagination.

After a spell as the Plaza shopping mall, the Bourne & Hollingsworth building is now a large branch of Next.

Pioneering Women

Margaret Bondfield

Starting work aged 14 at a drapery in Hove, Sussex, 'Maggie' soon discovered that being a 'servant of the counter' was a position ripe for exploitation, especially through the 'living-in' system, and she became an active member of the shopworkers' union.

Margaret G. Bondfield

In 1896 she joined the Women's Industrial Council as an undercover agent called 'Grace Dare', on a two-year investigation into squalid shop conditions, taking jobs all over Britain, including a West End department store – 'a high-class shop (but one of the worst)'. By 1908 she was campaigning for independence, shorter hours and better pay.

In 1929 Margaret Bondfield became Minister for Labour: the first woman elected to the UK cabinet.

Ida Annie Fowle

Ida joined Harrods as 'second ledger clerk' in 1885 – the first woman to be employed by Charles Digby Harrod, the founder's son, who had hitherto refused to recruit women, claiming that men were more efficient and loyal. 'Several of the junior members of the staff peered round showcases to see the "beauty chorus" arrive,' she recalled of her first day.

Resilient, tactful and considerate, she was soon put in charge of the sales ledger section. Her hours were 8am to 8pm (10pm on Saturdays), with only two hours off one evening a week. As Harrods boomed, Miss Fowle's band of female clerks grew to 400, becoming known as 'Fowle's Chicks'. She ruled her brood for 36 years as Head Clerk of the Counting House, helping a flood of women pursue their dream of entering the 'lighter' areas of shopwork.

DRAGES 230 High Holborn, WC1, then 73–77 Oxford Street, W1 • 1908-1937

If you couldn't afford Shoolbreds or Waring & Gillows (and plenty couldn't), then you went to Drages. This home furnishing business flourished during the boom in hire purchase during the inter-war years, with business conducted largely on credit. Drages advertised in the *Daily Mail* rather than *Vogue*. 'Don't lead us into extravagance, Jane!', 'two young things' begged their sales assistant, in a typical example. They were delighted to discover the safety net of Drages' instalment payment system.

There was huge inter-war demand for new furniture, driven by the rise in affordable housing.

"To 25 Years of Happiness!"

Jane and John

DRAGES
for fine furniture

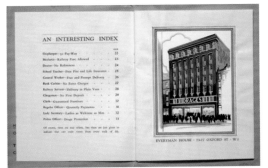

Hire purchase brought these dreams within reach, legitimised by clever advertising promoting furniture as part of an aspirational lifestyle. 'All Classes Furnish at Drage's' went the slogan (but it was delivered to your home in a plain van, so the neighbours didn't know you were buying on HP).

Benjamin Drage was a Jewish entrepreneur indifferent to British snobbery. Sensing a market,

he opened his store next to High Holborn Tube in 1908 and set about taking on the lower classes. His unique selling point wasn't the furniture, but himself. 'When you visit London look in and see Mr Drage,' went the advertisements, showing a fictionalised twinkling, affable gent. 'I regard customers as friends, rather than entries in a ledger.'

The innovative 'Mr Everyman' campaign, launched in 1922, featured a conversation between the ebullient Mr Drage and Mr or Mrs Everyman. For various legitimate reasons, Mr Everyman was short on cash.

DRAGES FINE FURNITURE
Do you realise...?

SO PAY-WAY TERMS

LAST WEEK of DRAGES SALE

DRAGES
73-77 OXFORD STREET, LONDON, W.1
FREE

Perhaps he was an officer who'd lost his home during the war, or a man about to get married. He (or she) was thrilled by the terms on offer at Drages. An ad in the *John Bull* newspaper, 1927, has Mr Everyman exclaiming, 'You mean what you say, Mr Drage. 4 years' credit and no deposit!'

The Everyman branding extended to the new flagship store on Oxford Street, designed in 1929 by Gordon Jeeves and Herbert Welch in polished grey granite with wavy pink mouldings in white brass – one of Oxford Street's finest examples of the Modernist Style. Named 'Everyman House', this was 'a munificent store for the service of that increasingly exuberant pair, Mr and Mrs Everyman.' Its opening – Drage's twenty-first birthday – was celebrated with a cake weighing nearly four tons and distributed, 'fifty thousand pieces, all in charming boxes,' to its customers. Branches in Birmingham and Manchester opened around the same time.

The 'Mr Everyman' campaign became a bit of national joke, featuring in a 1925 musical hall song, 'The Drage Way'. Mr Everyman is 'on the rocks and broke' because his new wife has been shopping.

So five hundred pounds of furniture, she spent, did my old Dutch; 'What deposit, Mr Drage,' said I, 'would you require for such?' He simply smiled and said, 'Would two and sixpence be too much?' And we'll always lay your lino on the floor!'

I said, 'That's very generous, but no reference I've got.' He said, 'We do not want them, they're a lot of tommy rot. Why, you needn't give your name, if you would rather not, And we'll always lay your lino on the floor!'

The problem with hire purchase was that it left businesses without capital and vulnerable to bad debts. Drages was taken over by the Drapery Trust in 1928, sold with debts to Great Universal Stores in 1937, and liquidated soon afterwards. Its superb Art Deco building survived on Oxford Street until 2014, when it was controversially demolished. At least its wavy pink brass cladding was successfully salvaged.

SHOOLBREDS 154–156 Tottenham Court Road, W1 • 1817-1934

The name of this department store lives on today through its furniture. Those little ivorine labels, discreetly screwed beneath or behind, have become a talisman for antique dealers and collectors the world over. 'JAMES SHOOLBRED & Co, Tottenham House, Tottenham Court Road, LONDON' speaks of superior British craftsmanship, and a certain snob cachet.

Shoolbreds once counted among Britain's most distinctive exports. The firm exhibited at the 1853 New York Exhibition, then at the 1876 Philadelphia Centennial exhibition, taking the Americans on an irresistible tour of British upper-class style. Six

interior designed rooms showcased the Jacobean, Queen Anne and Anglo-Indian styles, with an excursion into 'Italian Renaissance'. At the 1878 Paris Exposition, some 13 million visitors passed before their room displays – the walnut and rosewood library; the dining-room suite in gleaming satinwood; the bedroom furniture in inlaid teak. In 1885 Shoolbreds' triumph in Paris was recognised with a Royal Warrant.

It all started in 1817, when a Scottish linen draper, James (Jas) Shoolbred, opened a store on Tottenham Court Road supplying textiles to the furniture trade. By the 1860s the company was designing, manufacturing and selling its own sophisticated furniture in its thriving store, expanding then relocating to the corner of Tottenham Court Road and

University Street, Bloomsbury. Here, customers would be greeted with a bowing, frock-coated doorman and served with discreet unctuousness by one of 500 staff. Nowhere else in London could you find everything essential to the upper-class Victorian home under one roof, from sanitary ware to Persian carpets.

Thirty years later, Shoolbreds had evolved to serve the burgeoning middle classes with all manner of goods, from whisky to carriage clocks, cigars to corsets. 'The World's Shopping Centre', proclaimed a double-page advertisement in the *Illustrated London News*, 1910: 'Eighty Big Shops in One'. Away from the smarter end of Oxford Street and exclusive Regent Street, 'The very highest value at the very lowest cost'

appealed to the bowler-hatted clerks and office workers of Bloomsbury, as well as to their wives. Mr Pooter's wife Carrie buys a white fan from Shoolbreds for three and sixpenny in *The Diary of a Nobody* (1892). The store was one of the first to stock off-the-peg 'tailor-made' suits and blouses for women, a trend disparaged by

upper-class consumers.

The great financial crisis of the Twenties, together with the boom in mass manufacturing, was to prove traumatic. In 1927 Shoolbreds was advertising corsetry for the 'Full Figure' – 'Youth-line Reduso'. In 1928 it gamely put on an exhibition of 'Modern Furniture'. But in 1931 Harrods swooped, buying the stock and the firm's goodwill. Tottenham House was closed in 1934 and the merchandise sold off.

Furniture aside, one intriguing item from this era remains intact: a gilt-painted, mahogany memorial to the Shoolbreds men who fought in the Great War. It's unusual in carrying names of the 519 men who saw action and survived, as well as the 26 who died at the Somme. Recently restored, it now hangs in the ground

floor stairwell of Paramount Court, the landmark Art Deco block of flats built on the Shoolbred site.

It's fascinating that the men's commanding officer was a Shoolbred: Lt Col. Rupert Wilkin Shoolbred, remembered for his paternalistic concern for both workers and horses before, during and after the war. The department store's fleet of horses, used to pull its delivery vans, was requisitioned for the Front.

STAGG & MANTLE   Leicester Square, WC2 • 1812–1949

Stagg & Mantle seems, more than others, to belong to an archaic era. Its customers were solidly Victorian, and its location meant it also dressed actors, music hall stars and opera singers (it had a long association with the Royal Opera House). Leicester Square was renowned for its pickpockets: arrests under the store's awnings were common. Hundreds of ambitious young men cut and thrust their way up the Stagg & Mantle career ladder during the mid- to late-nineteenth-century, when the drapery world was still male-dominated. The dream was to leave and open a rival enterprise nearby – and then, who knows? Peter Jones did an apprenticeship here, before setting up on his own in Chelsea, 1871.

Leicester Square's own department store did its best to keep pace with the times. In 1926 it staged a show of 'exclusive Paris Fashions' at the opulent new Capitol Theatre on Haymarket ('London's latest super-cinema'), promoting the premiere of a Howards Hawks silent movie, *Fig Leaves*, featuring a technicolour fashion show sequence.

In 1930, famous shop fitters Frederick Sage gave Stagg & Mantle a row of beautiful, curved glass window cabinets in mahogany and bronze, Art-Deco style. But their displays lacked the élan of Oxford and Regent Street's, and customers increasingly travelled west for fashion. In 1949 the store went into voluntary liquidation, and was absorbed into the Burton group.

Daring to Strike for Their Rights

In 1919, the biggest retail strike in British history brought the Army & Navy to its knees. Over 3,000 employees walked out on Wednesday 3 December, protesting over archaic working conditions and pay. Customers that morning were indignant to find no

commissionaire dog minders at the entry to the Stores: a sign that all was not well within.

The three-day strike was masterminded by Philip Hoffman: former draper's assistant and prime mover within the Shop Assistants' Union (founded 1891). Hoffman had himself experienced the A&N's arcane pettiness as a youth. 'When you applied to enter the service of the Stores

MONDAY, 8 DECEMBER, 1919.

STRIKE WINNERS' SMILES.—The higher wages for which the [A&N] and [Navy] hands stopped work were granted, and they received full pay for the [strike] period.

you filled up a form,' he remembered. 'And such a form! Some of the questions were: Who were your last four employers? Have you had varicose veins? Have you ever had fits?' He learned that employees were required to leave pipe, tobacco and matches in a bag at the staff entrance. That they were liable to be searched on their exit. That there were fines for borrowing, lending and gambling, possession of matches or an indelible pencil. All this, for derisory wages.

By 1919, saleswomen in one department averaged

22 shillings a week. A foreman of 42 years service got 47s. A girl cashier taking £50 a day got 8s a week, and if one penny was short she'd be fined 6d. The workers were demanding a 35 per cent pay rise, a 44-hour week, payment for overtime and holidays, and wages during illness. The short-lived strike gained overwhelming public support – not least when it was revealed that the military founders' shares were repaying at 350 per cent. Demands were conceded, and the great wheels of the store were humming again by Saturday morning.

The Army & Navy strike laid the groundwork for a London-wide agreement between department stores. Four months later, staff at the punitively autocratic John Lewis followed suit, in what would become a six-week strike. But the curmudgeonly, white bearded John Lewis refused to budge, sacking the 400 strikers on the spot, most of them young women. Rival stores, including Harrods and the Army & Navy, supported the striking workers, who wanted simply to be allowed to join the Shop Workers Union. After six fruitless weeks they called the strike off – and were snapped up by Pontings of Kensington, whose manager was delighted to get 'quality' shopgirls.

'We are living in a different age than that of five years ago. Not only must we be paid more but we must be allowed to do what we like with our leisure time. Wage earners are not slaves now, they are human beings who have some rights and a claim to consideration. The Union is our protection. Mr Lewis has his solicitors – we must have our Union.'

Miss Hilda Canham, John Lewis strike leader

THE CIVIL SERVICE SUPPLY ASSOCIATION

4–6 Bedford Street and 425 Strand, WC2 – 'The Strand Stores'
136 Queen Victoria Street, EC2 – 'The City Store' • 1866–1982

They were known as 'the Stores', and, while each had its idiosyncrasies, all four shared the same goal. The Army & Navy, the Junior Army & Navy, the Civil Service Supply Association and the Civil Service Cooperative Association were all there to save members money. Rival West End department stores were hit hard by the inexorable growth of the co-operative model; in 1880 Harrods began advertising 'co-operative prices,' and other traders followed suit.

Belonging to one of London's Stores conferred a sense of identity; it was a private club where you felt at home. Aspiring members needed an introduction from an elected member, a ticket from the Store Secretary (price 2s 6d), and the strict understanding that 'all

purchases would be negotiated for cash'. Then you were in.

Was membership of the Stores worth it, on grounds of economy alone? Charles Eyre Pascoe, author of the Society handbook *London of To-Day* (1890-92) thought not. The Civil Service Supply Association's City headquarters on Queen Victoria Street he found particularly exasperating. 'No more perplexing labyrinth irritating to nerves and temper, and wasteful of time, could be entered, at least by a busy man.' One hour could be spent in 'trying to save a couple of shillings'. The service was austere: the customer had to consult the price list, fill in an invoice for each department's goods, make payment at the cashier's office, then queue at another counter to have the goods assembled.

Yet it was always seething with customers.

London's earliest co-operative association was formed by 40 impecunious London Post Office clerks clubbing together in 1864 to buy a chest of tea, in order to save ninepence a pound. Success led them to branch out into sugar and coffee; membership increased to 700. The following year the 'Post Office Supply Association' opened up to all civil servants, changing its name and gaining thousands of members.

Lockwood and Mawson's triumphant 'Roman Renaissance' building in red brick and terracotta (*The Builder* magazine, 1877).

CIVIL SERVICE STORES.

"WHAT CAN WE DO FOR YOU, MADAM? ROYAL COMMISSION?—SELECT COMMITTEE?—PAPERS?—CAREFUL CONSIDERATION?—OFFICIAL INQUIRY? ANYTHING TO OBLIGE!"

The Strand Art Deco building, 1930s.

By 1868, with 10,000 customers, a retail shop was opened in the Strand for groceries, then clothing and household goods. By 1870 the Civil Service Supply Association was boasting it could provide 'anything from a blotting-pad to a bicycle or a billiard table – from ginger beer to carte blanche champagne'.

At first, competing retailers were scornful of the business efforts of the 'notoriously incapable' civil servants, but within a year or two they became seriously alarmed. In 1868, a *Times* leader suggested that 'so rapid is the extension of this remarkable movement, that it threatens nothing less than a social revolution.'

Such huge success was a surprise to its Civil Service pioneers. Profits were beyond their wildest dreams. In 1872 'large and handsome' premises were found in the City on Queen Victoria Street, and two years later architects were engaged to create a brand-new building in the West End.

Architects Lockwood and Mawson were from Bradford, Yorkshire – a city with a prominent co-operative society since 1861 and (along with Rochdale) the inspiration behind the London movement. The duo were responsible for some of Bradford's most distinguished buildings, such as the City Hall and Wool Exchange, as well as creating Saltaire, Sir Titus Salt's model village in Shipley. The imposing red-brick and terracotta co-operative store opened in 1877 in Bedford Street in Covent Garden, once the site of a boot-blacking factory where Charles Dickens worked as a boy in 1824. In the interwar years the store moved down the street to an Art Deco building on the corner of the Strand.

CIVIL SERVICE CO-OPERATIVE SOCIETY
28 Haymarket, SW1 · 1866–1931

This rival organisation was set up in 1866, growing more slowly but steadily from premises known as the Haymarket Stores. Membership was initially for civil servants, but soon its 2s 6d annual tickets were available to peers, members of parliament, justices of the peace, army and naval officers, and clergymen.

Over in Brompton, Charles Digby Harrod was following this particular store's genesis with keen interest. In direct imitation, he branched out into perfumes, patent medicines and stationery in 1868; he also copied their pricing policies, such as selling branded items below the manufacturers' list prices – even using the slogan 'co-operative prices'.

CSCS members were issued with a fob to be shown at the door: a round, leather, burgundy-grained disk, inscribed with gilded script. On the back, an Arts and Crafts-inspired elaborate tangle of initials: CSCS.

The store flourished until 1931, when it was – ironically – taken over by Harrods and promptly closed.

Both CSSA premises still stand today, and strangely both were victims of serious fires, which gutted the period interior of Lockwood and Mawson's building and forced the closure of the Strand store for good. Until recently the Bedford Street premises housed a TGI Fridays restaurant, while the blue clock on the wall of the erstwhile Strand store is a striking relic of its former role.

Fighting for the Right to Rest

1842 – **Early Closing Association is formed** (shop assistants work a punishing 13-17 hour day, up to midnight on Saturdays, seven days a week).

The Peter Robinson canteen: 'a blend of the semi-monastic institution and strict boarding school'.

1877 – **Brixton's Bon Marché opens**, Britain's first purpose-built department store, with 50 staff bedrooms. Staff welfare rises up the agenda.

1884 – **Eight Hour League is formed**, an 8-hour working day its goal.

1886 – **Shop Hours Regulation Act**: children and young persons' work restricted to 72 hours a week.

1888 – **Defeated**: a Bill to restrict shop hours.

1891 – **Defeated**: a Bill proposing one half day a week for shop assistants.

1891 – **National Union of Shop Assistants is formed.**

1899 – **Seats for Shop Assistants Act** imposes 'temporary seating for women assistants' – but isn't enforced.

1901 – Thirteen male **shop assistants from Whiteleys parade Oxford Street** with sandwich boards advertising a mass meeting against 'living in'.

1902 – **Mass demonstration** of 1,000 shop assistants in Trafalgar Square demanding a 60-hour week.

1904 – **Shop Hours Act** empowers local authorities to fix their own shop hours, closing no earlier than 7pm.

1907 – The **'living in' agitation grows**. Two thirds of Britain's 750,000 shop workers are affected.

1912 – **Shops Act** introduces half-day early closing once a week (from 4pm). Peter Robinson is the last of the capital's department stores to make the transition to staff 'living out'.

1928 – **Compulsory Closing Act**: shops must now close at 8pm, one late night at 9pm.

Below: John Lewis shop assistants go on strike, 1920.

THE LEEDS MERCURY, WEDNESDAY, APRIL 28, 1920.

LONDON SHOP GIRLS' STRIKE—When a sale was to commence at a large London drapers, the shop assistants went on strike for better conditions. The result was that salesgirls were torn between the temptations of sale bargains and sympathy for the strikers. Above is a party of girl pickets taking up position outside the stores.

SIMPSON PICCADILLY 203–206 Piccadilly, W1 • 1936–1999

A fortnight before the grand opening of Simpson Piccadilly, 33-year-old Alec Simpson wrote yet another detailed letter to his architect Joseph Emberton.

> 10 April 1936:
> I went through the building yesterday evening and there appears to be such a lot still to be done. The finishing of the floors, odd bits of painting and decoration, carpets, furnishing, shop fitting and lighting, all seem to leave a lot to be done.

Daily for the past year he had been stalking the building site, fine-tuning the realisation of this revolutionary department store for men. 'I feel very much like the captain of a big new ship,' he wrote to his

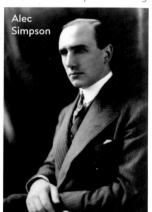

Alec Simpson

architect, 'waiting for the pilot in charge of the tugs to get him out of dock, so that I can sail spick and span on my maiden voyage.'

Alexander (Alec) Simpson was the William Whiteley or Harry Gordon Selfridge of his era. Catching the spirit of the Thirties, he enlisted new architecture, new materials, new fabrics, new ideas for display, marketing and advertising, and assembled them together in a bold and innovative store with a crystal-clear mission.

The Flying Flea: three aircraft were displayed on the fifth floor for the store's opening.

Simpson Piccadilly would be 'the greatest menswear store in the West End.' It would bring Savile Row tailoring to the department store – and so to the masses.

Simpson had tailoring in his blood. His father, Simeon Simpson, was a Victorian tailor who founded the House of Simpson at a time when new machinery was revolutionising the trade. The 'band-knife' now allowed many thicknesses of cloth to be cut simultaneously. Buttonholes could be sewed by

Menswear at this time was in transition. Ready-to-wear was expanding, while increased leisure time meant that sportswear was growing. Alec Simpson, a keen golfer, shared a common frustration that his shirt would ride up after every golf swing. He set about finding a solution. The result was the DAKS sports trouser, patented in 1932 with its self-supporting, rubber padded waistband – 'no braces or belt needed'. DAKS became a worldwide phenomenon . . . and Alec Simpson began to dream of a men's department store.

machine; steam pressing need no longer be done by hand. Alec joined the firm at 15 and learned on the job, travelling widely through Europe and the United States. When his father died suddenly in 1932, he became managing director. He was just 30.

In 1934 he bought a site on Piccadilly at auction for £11,000 on a 99-year lease, and

'A Commanding Officer forms his first impression from your uniform': Simpson's Uniform Department was quickly formed in 1939.

commissioned an English architect, Joseph Emberton, to design what would turn out to be Emberton's masterpiece.

Within Simpson's immense steel frame was a glass wall, rising the height of the building and filling each open-plan floor with natural light. A great staircase in Travertine

The Bauhaus artist László Moholy-Nagy designed uncluttered, modern interiors in light woods with paintwork in red, sky blue or emerald green.

marble spiralled up the centre. At street level front and back, distinctive, non-reflecting, concave windows were the first of their kind in Britain. Book-ended by Victorian buildings, Simpson Piccadilly screamed Modernism.

Inside, there would be theatre. Alec Simpson wanted a floor of tailors, cutters and pressers working away, in full view of customers. For this department to be buzzing on opening day, he had to persuade 50 friends to order suits for 12 to 14 guineas. 'Do you think you could favour me with an order, please?' he asked Emberton, with characteristic bluntness. 'I don't see that I shall be doing you a favour in buying a Simpson suit,' his architect replied. 'It is a thing I have been looking forward to for a long time.'

Four days later, traffic vibrations cracked the newly patented windows beside the main entrance, and the local authority insisted they were made safe with unsightly brown paper. Replacements were promised by the following Monday, with the store due to open two days later. Meanwhile, doorposts were being removed from the main entrance so that three light aircraft, including the 'Flying Flea', could be fitted through and hauled up to the fifth floor. Alec Simpson was ill with the strain, but he continued to obsessively tweak the

'Men, so rumour has it, dislike shopping,' wrote the Manchester *Guardian*'s correspondent. 'The aim of the founders of the new store is to create an atmosphere where men shall feel at home, where they may buy not only their own shirts and socks, but purchase silk stockings

for their womenfolk and presents for the family in a setting which is congenial and heartily male.' But would men fall for it? 'Only the future can tell whether the attempt will succeed, or whether women will invade this new store in much the same way as they have monopolised all others.'

store's interior design, overseen by Laszlo Moholy-Nagy, and fine-tune the advertising campaign, featuring lantern-jawed men by the Viennese artist Max Hoff.

Simpson Piccadilly was opened to plan on 29 April 1936 by the world land speed record holder, Sir Malcolm Campbell. VIPs admired the uncluttered, spare interiors; the chairs in modern bent plywood; the shirts displayed on plastic, heat-formed, body-shaped stands. Men's tailoring had been pepped up with an astonishing range of colours and fabrics. There was even modern American underwear in cotton (rather than woollen combinations with buttons down the front); Y-fronts with elasticated waistbands and trims.

A year after opening, as Simpson had planned, women's wear opened on the fourth floor. But just as Alec Simpson sent Joseph Emberton a five-page list

of more changes to be made, he was diagnosed with leukaemia. He died in May 1937, aged 34.

Simpson's 'big new ship' continued to sail (Alec's elder brother Samuel stepped into his shoes), becoming a brand that men would covet for the next 60 years. In 1992, the Queen popped in to buy Prince Philip a sweater. And yet what began as an exercise in cutting-edge design became a symbol of traditionalism – thanks to the famed politeness of its staff, the classic cut of its clothes, and the middle-aged customer base. Simpson Piccadilly inspired the TV sitcom *Are You Being Served?* (1972–84), which mocked the self-importance and petty politics of life behind the counter (co-writer Jeremy Lloyd worked here in the 1940s).

Eventually the languid, leisurely style of Simpsons became anachronistic – an ocean-going liner in a package tour age. With financial losses mounting, the site was sold to booksellers Waterstones in 1999 to become their flagship store. It remains a London landmark, Grade 1 listed, testimony to one man's bold vision. As *Art and Industry* summed up at

the store's 1936 opening, 'Hats off to Mr Alec Simpson – for, whatever may be said about his store, it is a brave adventure.'

SWAN & EDGAR Piccadilly Circus, W1 • 1812–1982

On a wet Friday evening on the first day of March 1912, the sound of shattering glass rang throughout London's West End. 'Shortly before six o'clock a band of women carried out such a window-breaking campaign in the principal streets of the West End as London has never known,' reported the *Daily Telegraph*. In less than an hour, a closely choreographed wave of Suffragette militancy smashed nearly 400 shop windows, causing some £5,000-worth of damage. The glittering window displays were plunged into darkness. Swan & Edgar, on its prime position on Piccadilly Circus, was at the centre of the melée.

One week later, the store was advertising fur coats in the Suffragette newspaper *Votes for Women*. Swan & Edgar wasn't going to lose its most valuable female customers, whatever Emmeline Pankhurst's frustrations with the Liberal government. Neighbouring victims of the attack – Marshall & Snelgrove, D. H. Evans, Jays, Liberty, Robinson & Cleaver – followed suit.

On 14 June 1913, the Suffragettes were out in force again for the funeral procession of 40-year-old Emily Wilding Davison, trampled beneath the King's horse on Derby day. The black hearse passed before Swan & Edgar, through a thronged Piccadilly Circus, on its way up Shaftesbury Avenue to St George's, Bloomsbury. Six thousand women, elegantly dressed in black, purple and white, marched slowly behind.

Swan & Edgar's location has made it, perforce, a witness to history. On the night of 17 October 1917, a German Zeppelin dropped a 300kg bomb on Piccadilly Circus, smashing the store's entire façade. Five men and two women were killed; 18 more waiting for a bus were wounded. The bomb blew a hole right down to the store's cellars.

Who hasn't waited for a bus at Piccadilly Circus, perhaps right by this very spot? Edwardian shopper *par excellence* 'Olivia' writes in her 1906 shopping guide that when

'The argument of the broken pane of glass' – Emmeline Pankhurst, 1912.

finding herself in this predicament, she happily distracts herself with Swan & Edgar's windows – the biggest and 'most comprehensive' in Regent Street. 'Everything of consequence is in them, including the prices, and many times the waiting for an omnibus has shown me a much-sought article lying there ready to be bought.'

The shop front has had many different faces since the store's beginnings in 1812. George Swan and William Edgar, haberdashers, were forced to move premises to 49 Regent Street when their bow-fronted shop was demolished for the creation of Piccadilly Circus. Swan died in 1821 but Edgar kept the name, expanding into neighbouring shops until, in 1848, he commanded the entire corner of the street. 'Swan & Edgar's Corner' was formalised in gold letters over the Circus-facing shop front. It was a favourite meeting spot – then, and throughout the store's subsequent incarnations.

In 1910, the Crown Estate issued a diktat that all facades had to be classically designed in Portland stone. Sir Reginald Blomfield was pulled in to redevelop Regent Street's Quadrant – but the new building lasted only until that fateful Zeppelin raid. The subsequent 1920s rebuild was entrusted to Scottish architects Louis David Blanc (who worked in-house for Harrods) and John James Joass (joint architect for Whiteley's 1911 reconstruction). Joass created a long, low light well running through the centre of the store, with a fireproof ceiling of amber Cristol glass – the first of its kind.

The new premises opened with a fanfare of publicity in June 1927, a year before the reconstructed Piccadilly Circus Tube station opened with its Art Deco underground ticket hall and 11 escalators. 'In the new Swan & Edgar Building, over fifty Merchandise and Service Departments supply every need for Men, Women and Children. You are cordially invited to inspect the perfectly appointed salons and to visit the delightful Restaurant, admittedly the finest in its kind in the country.' Delightfully modern it might have been, but Saturday closing remained fixed at 1 p.m. The Shops Act of 1911 had enshrined a weekly half-holiday for staff, a law that wouldn't be repealed until 1994.

The grand façade with its three wide bays became a distinctive landmark; a failsafe rendezvous. In 1952, *Picture Post* sent the photojournalist Daniel Farson to lurk behind the statue of Eros and train his lens on the store's frontage. 'Meet Me Outside' is a story of snatched, intimate moments; of assignations made or missed. 'Peak hours for meetings are lunch time and six-ish in the evening,' wrote Farson, 'but there is always a nucleus of fluctuating hope and dismal anxiety. Although doubt is usually happily resolved, there is always the girl who stalks off to a solitary Welsh rarebit, or the man who strolls away with brave unconcern, pretending he'd rather spend the evening with the boys anyway.'

Swan & Edgar was acquired by Harrods in 1920, then in 1927 by the Drapery Trust, which in turn became part of the Debenhams Group in the 1970s. It closed in 1982 after 170 years of retail. Three years later the building was taken over by the American record chain Tower Records for its London flagship – but record stores have since outpaced department stores almost into outright extinction.

When Hitler Came to Oxford Street

On the night of Tuesday, 17 September 1940, the Luftwaffe visited the capital in a raid of intense ferocity. Oxford Street was the target. A river of fire burned the length of the 'Golden Mile', from Tottenham Court

Selfridges, D. H. Evans, Bourne & Hollingsworth and Peter Robinson. The work of generations of retailers and architects had been obliterated overnight. Thirty fire engines were called in to tackle the blaze; crews struggled until Friday to bring the flames under control.

Bourne & Hollingsworth (left)
Two 500-pound bombs gouged a huge hole in B&H's interior, littering the surrounding streets with shards of glass. But in the spirit of the Blitz, staff returned to work the next day and patriotically hid the damage by unfurling a series of large Union flags over the storefront. A week later, part of the store's eastern wing was reopened for business.

D. H. Evans

Despite a direct hit, it was business as usual for this great store in its modernist incarnation (1937). 'Many of the counters were blown in,' a staff member told the *Yorkshire Evening Post*, 'but we are seeing what can be done to start the day's work.' Hundreds of sales girls had already arrived to begin work, as fires still raged beyond Oxford Circus. 'They sat calmly in the basement awaiting orders, while firemen still played their hoses on the debris nearby.'

Road to Marble Arch, as a steady stream of bombers whined overhead. The raging fires acted as a reference point for new waves of Luftwaffe, unleashing yet more damage on the household names below.

When dawn broke on 18 September, five of the West End's most prestigious department stores were either ablaze, badly damaged or destroyed: John Lewis,

John Lewis

The emporium's neo-classical West House was hit by an oil bomb, showering the building with burning oil and petrol. Fire spread rapidly across Holles Street to destroy most of the East House (a tunnel-linked extension built in 1928). While both were reduced to fire-scorched shells, 200 sheltering in the basements escaped unhurt. Staff salvaged what they could from the rubble and John Lewis struggled back to its feet.

Three weeks later, part of the East House was reopened for business.

When George Orwell walked past the smouldering John Lewis bombsite, he noted that the mannequins piled up outside looked disconcertingly like corpses. Fellow war journalist Kingsley Amis described the remnants of this once grand department store as 'like the ruins of a Greek temple'.

Peter Robinson

The upper section of the building's neo-classical façade was ripped open; three floors were destroyed; plate glass windows and debris were blown into Oxford Circus. Parts of Peter Robinson were reopened four days later, but its Oxford Circus storefront was boarded up and subsequently used to display war advertising hoardings.

Selfridges' Palm Court restaurant completely destroyed.

Selfridges

A single high-explosive bomb hit Selfridges, along with several incendiaries. Harry Gordon Selfridge, 84, wept to see his prized signature window, autographed by dozens of celebrity visitors since 1909, shattered in the blast. The elegant roof gardens were also badly damaged, never to open again. After the raid, the famous ground-floor windows were bricked up for the war's duration.

The Blitz Spirit

• Central London's department stores made a 'chain gang' pact, sharing staff canteens and restrooms with their competitors in the event of air-raid damage.

• Selfridges' blackout accessories included a range of goods aimed at increasing human and canine visibility in the dark. White raincoats, luminous flower brooches, little blackout coats for dogs . . .

• By mid-1943 some 90 per cent of single women and 80 per cent of married women were working for the war effort. Department stores were forced to fill the employment gap with teenagers, the elderly and married women (many doubling up as in-house air raid wardens). This moment marked a shift from shop girls to shop women.

JOHN BARNES 191–217 Finchley Road, NW3 • 1900-1981

Skewered octopus, Russian mushrooms, Greek figs, Spanish paella . . . all these and more could be found in the famous John Barnes food hall by the 1930s. Fondly known as 'Johan Barnes' by Swiss Cottage's German Jewish refugees, the store was, in the end, almost cannibalised by the success of its food department. In 1952 John Barnes was the first to offer

Front View of Barnes Store, Finchley Road, N.W.

self-service. People would travel miles across London for its exotic delicacies – which, by 1953, could be delivered to you on holiday, 'whether camp, caravan, houseboat or bungalow'. Whatever your story, John Barnes' food hall offered a taste of home.

It also offered a whole lot more. Unlike most British department stores, which grew from small beginnings, this was conceived on a grand scale right from its start. Five shrewd retail veterans gathered to pool their expertise: Owen Owen of Liverpool, William Jones of Jones Brothers in Holloway, John Jones of Regent Street's Dickins & Jones, Edwin Jones of Bon Marché

in Brixton and the chairman John Barnes, of Barker's in Kensington.

Swiss Cottage, with its growing population and good transport links, was ripe for investment. A long block of properties was acquired, big enough to comfortably house 400 staff in accommodation 'which would do credit to a first-class hotel'. The shop floors were more lavish still: Axminster carpet, a central lift and the new Lamson pneumatic tube system to save delays at cash desks. (At the time only three other stores had the Lamson: Bon Marché, Robinson & Cleaver and Roberts of Stratford).

Chairman John Barnes never got to see his great project through to completion. In 1899 he was drowned at sea when the passenger steamship *Stella* ran aground off Guernsey. A year later to the day, John Barnes department store opened on Finchley Road, named in tribute to the missing partner.

Takings that first year totalled almost £125,000 – equivalent to over £10 million today. By 1926, an impressed Gordon Selfridge had acquired John Barnes as one of his Selfridge Provincial Stores. Under Selfridge's eye the entire store was given a 1930s rebuild by the architect T. P. Bennett (later responsible for the new towns of Crawley and Stevenage), emerging in 1935 as a sleek and gleaming modernist building. The new store had eight storeys: three floors for the store, five for flats above.

But just as the new John Barnes took shape on Finchley Road, Selfridge's empire was collapsing. The struggling Provincial Store group, now reduced to 16

John Barnes' famous food basement went self-service in 1952: it was one of London's first.

shops, was sold to the John Lewis Partnership in 1940. John Barnes emerged unscathed from the war, spared by the bombs, mopping up the trade of those less fortunate. But it couldn't contend with Brent Cross. When Britain's first indoor regional shopping centre opened just three miles away in 1976, the impact was catastrophic. Shoppers now visited John Barnes for its food hall alone. And it wasn't enough.

Finchley Road's proud department store finally closed its doors in 1981. More happily, the ground floor is today the thriving 'Waitrose John Barnes' food hall.

JONES BROTHERS
348–356 Holloway Road, N7 • 1867–1990

In 1910, a sensational trial at the Old Bailey hinged on a pair of Jones Brothers striped cotton pyjamas. They belonged to the murderous Dr Crippen, who had used them to wrap up the body of his wife Corinne.

THE MOST SENSATIONAL TRIAL FOR MANY YEARS: THE CRIPPEN CASE.

THE HEARING OF THE CHARGE AGAINST HAWLEY HARVEY CRIPPEN: SKETCHES IN COURT.

GH 1 PYJAMA SUITS, in good quality Ceylonette.

Crippen, a shady American homeopath, was accused of killing her after starting an affair with a young typist, Ethel Le Neve. His wife's torso was found under the floorboards of the couple's home, 39 Hilldrop Crescent, together with a crucial piece of evidence: a scrap of striped pyjama bearing the label 'Shirtmakers Jones Bros (Holloway) Ltd'.

The Crippens were regulars at their local department store, particularly during the sales. Corinne had bought the pyjamas in the 1909 January sale: in court, menswear buyer James Chilvers produced the receipt. That all-important 'Ltd' on the label proved that the pyjamas were not (as Crippen argued) from a far earlier era, which would have meant the body was nothing to do with him. Jones Brothers had become a limited company in 1906. On this vital shred of evidence, Dr Crippen was to hang.

Some eighty years later, Jones Brothers made headlines again, with the shocking announcement of its closure in 1990 by the John Lewis Partnership (who had acquired the business from Selfridge Provincial Stores in 1940). 'Save Jones Brothers' posters went up the length of the Holloway Road. Hundreds of locals linked arms around the store in angry protest. The department store was (and always had been) dear to residents, many of them unable or unwilling to shop elsewhere. Thousands signed petitions, withdrew their accounts from John Lewis and wrote furious letters.

The JLP was adamant. The Victorian building was,

they claimed, 'worn out'. It wasn't profitable enough. The Partnership was accused of cravenly focusing its resources on the out-of-town shopping centre, Brent Cross, and its flagship stores on Oxford Street and Sloane Square. One local MP, Chris Smith, summed up their decision as 'arrogantly dismissive of local feelings and local people'.

Another, Jeremy Corbyn (Islington North), brought the story of Jones Brothers before the Commons. If it closed, he argued, 'We will then be left with a run-down, boarded-up shopping area alongside a major road on which much traffic hurtles through.

The people of that community will be the losers, as will the 500 people who work in Jones Brothers. That will be a sad day.'

Corbyn's speech was prophetic, but fortunately not of the fate of Jones Brothers. The JLP converted its modern extension into a Waitrose, and the rest of the store – founded by a Welsh-speaking draper from Caernarfonshire – is still a handsome landmark on the Holloway Road. Today it's a conference centre for the charity sector.

GAMAGES 116–128 Holborn, EC1 • 1878–1972

When Arthur Gamage died aged 74 in 1930, he lay royally in state on a catafalque in the department store's Motoring Department, with members of staff acting guard

THE PRINCE OF "CUTTERS"

Mr. A. W. GAMAGE

day and night. This grand exit summed up the characterful impresario who lived, breathed and died for his store. It was a religion, an obsession. Gamage had spent the last half-century walking around his multifarious departments – touching, improving, encouraging, reproving; searching the globe for the best and the latest; selling fine goods at tight margins for the pleasure of millions.

'Tall Oaks from Little Acorns Grow' was the motto nailed above Arthur Gamage's modest hosiery business, opened in unfashionable Holborn in 1878. The store that measured just five feet across would grow in time to become 'the People's Popular Emporium' – and Whiteley's most serious rival. Arthur Gamage's trading

rationale was simple: undercut the competition, even if this made him 'the best-hated man in the retail trade'.

His first coup was to cram his window display with the latest craze: rubber-cushioned hairbrushes. Other shops sold them at 2/6d; Gamage sold his at 1/6d. He quickly sold out. How was he able to sell the brushes so cheaply? 'By buying right,' came the quick reply.

For the rest of his life, Gamage single-mindedly sought out small manufacturers and ordered directly from them – 'the only way get the lowest figures' for his customers. Since the store was close to the City and Fleet Street, the majority of these customers were men: bank clerks, office workers and messenger boys. If you wanted a cricket bat or a golf club, a football jersey or a strong man's leotard, a bicycle or a Boy

The Zoological Department claimed to be 'the largest and most complete in London'. Here you could buy parrots and cockatoos, a Grey Indian mongoose (good for rat-catching), a porcupine, chimpanzee or English hedgehog. Some 40 species of reptile were on offer, including 12-inch alligators. Rudyard Kipling remembered buying pet fish from a pool near the Grocery Department, served by 'a stern woman' who said she liked 'Nat'ral 'ist'ry'.

Scout uniform, you went to Gamages. And if you didn't live nearby, the store's catalogues offered every conceivable product, from bee-keeping equipment to bunion cream.

Within three years, Gamage had bought out his partner and begun acquiring neighbouring properties.

By 1890, he owned most of the block between Leather Lane and Hatton Garden. Navigating the store's warren of spaces was like being lost in a maze, but the disorientating experience added to the sense of exploration and the store's sense of identity. There was always a surprise just around the corner.

Both Arthur Gamage and his son, Eric, were mad about toys. These became the store's speciality. Arthur was famously dogged in tracking down unusual toys, enduring a blizzard in Chicago to find the maker of an ingenious toy gun; getting frostbitten ears on the way to a Novelties Fair in Chicago; searching for two days off the beaten track in Austria to find the maker of a toy he had spied in a shop window in Vienna.

Like a tenacious detective, Gamage invariably got his man or woman.

In Germany, he secured rights to Märklin toy locomotives (established 1859). In the Black Forest he persuaded Margarete Steiff (founder of Steiff, 1880) to sign over rights to her soft toy range which, from 1904, included the famous teddy bear. Gamages' unrivalled regiments of toy lead soldiers came from William

Britain in London's Hornsey Rise. The store had its own toy repair shop.

A former customer, remembering his visits from the East End in the early 1950s, likened it to 'an Aladdin's Cave'. 'Gamages was THE toy store,' writes Charles

Jenkins. 'Every child would look forward to a visit there. Families from all over the place would take buses to High Holborn. The kids, already hyped up, would jump off the bus with glee and dance along the street with excitement in the direction of the store. Their anticipation would reach almost breaking point as they dragged their parents along with increasing speed.' Thousands visited every Christmas just to gaze at the large model railway, which switched between day and night with ingenious lighting.

Magic was another Gamages speciality. A renowned magician, Will Goldston, ran the Magic and Entertainment departments from 1905 to 1914. If you wanted to hire 'England's favourite conjurer and ventriloquist' Stanley Collins for your party, with his upturned, flyaway moustache, or perhaps H. Hewson-Brown, 'the popular Dickens Impersonator,' you went to Gamages.

For many children, the arrival of the Gamages catalogue through the post was the first sign that Father Christmas was on his way. At the store itself, the toy department began its annual transformation into the 'world's most famous Christmas bazaar'. Late on Christmas Eve one year, Arthur Gamage received a telephone call at his home from a mother, distressed that the rocking horse she'd ordered for her son hadn't arrived. Early on Christmas morning, Gamage went to his store, collected the rocking horse and a Santa Claus outfit, and personally delivered the present in costume. In Gamages' Christmas catalogue the Santa Claus costume is described as being 'made up of cheap materials but has the desired effect'. So it seems.

Gamages was still a profitable enterprise in 1970 when it was acquired by property investors Sterling Guarantee Trust. The entire store was closed down and the building demolished to be replaced by a mirror-glass-clad skyscraper. Another branch was briefly opened on Oxford Street from the former Waring & Gillow building, but had shut again by 1972, prompting much nostalgia in the national press.

Back and Forth at a Rate of Knots

Revolving doors, off-the-peg suits, plate-glass windows, electric lighting, ladies' lavatories . . . the story of the big store is one of both perpetual reinvention – and the fear of change.

The innovators were found often in surprising quarters: Bon Marché of Brixton, John Barnes of Finchley. Others were resolutely stick-in-the-mud, valued eventually for their quaintness – such as Randalls of Uxbridge, the 1930s time capsule with its original cash desk and pneumatic tube system even into the twenty-first century.

One famous dinosaur was Charles Digby Harrod,

Harrods' moving conveyor belt, with smelling salts for those overcome by the experience.

son of the emporium's founder, who stubbornly resisted modern gadgetry such as electric lighting and overhead cash carriers. Yet by the 1890s, when all other department stores were installing lifts, his refusal led to an in-house invention that pioneered the escalator.

The Harrods' moving conveyor belt connected just two floors at an incline, with an attendant stationed at the top ready with smelling salts and brandy for those 'overcome with joy'. It opened in 1898 to a blaze of publicity. 'Such a getting upstairs there was yesterday

as has not been seen hitherto attempted in this country,' reported the *Pall Mall Gazette*. 'The novelty

Simpson Piccadilly gives the impression of total simplicity, but it was packed full of hidden innovations – such as a vacuum system to clean the whole building, consisting of a vertical vacuum tube installed from basement to roof with 'plug-in' cleaning tubes on each floor to carry the dirt downwards. Unfortunately the cleaners found the tubes too heavy to wield, so it quickly became redundant.

consists in an adaptation of the magic carpet of the fairy tale to the prosaic purpose of stairs.'

Cash: balls, cars and tubes

As stores expanded, tetchy customers had to wait up to half an hour while the sales assistant wrote out an order form, then sent a junior to the counting house with the money and form, returning at a run with change and a receipt. So when the Massachusetts inventor William Lamson sent an agent to London in 1884, British retailers began, cautiously, to adopt his American solutions.

First came the Cash Ball System, where cash was conveyed in hollow wooden balls running along a pair of inclined tracks – but the balls had a habit of falling off the track and smashing the glass counter below. Then, the Rapid Wire System: little cash-carrying cars running along fixed wires like

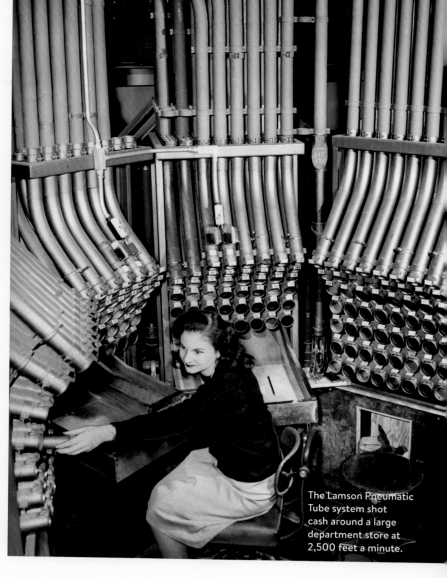

The Lamson Pneumatic Tube system shot cash around a large department store at 2,500 feet a minute.

miniature cable cars on a Swiss mountain. The assistant pulled the cord with a 'Ping!' and the car shot off. This was the system used by Barkers of Kensington, as one 1950s customer remembers: 'The cashier sat high up in a pulpit affair in the centre of the shop, and the carriers whizzed back and forth at a rate of knots.'

The turn-of-the-century Lamson Pneumatic Tube System was more costly but quieter, invisible and five times faster, the cylinders travelling at 2,500 feet a minute. Brixton's Bon Marché, Robinson & Cleaver of Regent Street and Roberts of Stratford were the first to install it. When the ultra-modern John Barnes opened on Finchley Road in 1900, it joined their number. A large emporium might need 16–18 miles of tubing.

Cash and invoices were folded into a cylinder that was placed into a vacuum tube, whisked up to the accounts floor, recorded by the cashiers and sent back down the tube with a receipt and change, a whoosh and a clank. It was a cumbersome system but it endured, intriguing generations of children who – to this day – remember craning their necks at the system of tubes or little carriages on rails above them. Many survived in department stores beyond the 1950s, long after the arrival of the cash register. Jacksons of Reading, which was late to install the Lamson Tube in the 1940s, was still using it in 2013 at its closure – allegedly the last store in the world to do so.

Lifts: a world within a world

'Parties who are old, fat, feeble, short-winded or simply lazy, or who desire a bit of fun, have only to place themselves on an enclosed platform . . .'

Selfridges' female lift attendants (pictured in 1928) later lost their jobs to disabled ex-servicemen.

Britain's first department store lift, 'a very ingenious hoisting apparatus', was installed at furnishers Wylie & Lochhead's in Glasgow in 1855. Fortunately, things became more streamlined – so much so that a lift

The first hydraulic passenger lift in England was installed at the Junior Army & Navy store in about 1880. Barbers of Fulham didn't get around to fitting a lift until 1988. It was used for just six years.

Present in most big department stores by 1900, lifts were grouped far away from the entrances, thus compelling customers to 'move through' the stores past the costly goods on the main floor.

installed in Selfridges in 1928 is today on show at the Museum of London. It wasn't just the technology that improved (brakes, hydraulics, the American Otis lift system from the 1880s onwards), but the revelation that the elevator itself could be an aesthetic thing of wonder, a world within a world.

Selfridges' series of bronze and cast-iron lifts, installed to mark its twentieth anniversary in 1929, featured glowing interior metal panels depicting cranes designed by Edgar William Brandt; the exterior screens consist of the signs of the zodiac by the Birmingham Guild of Metalworkers. The skilled designer, Walter Gilbert, was also creating Deco flourishes for Derry & Toms' fabulous rebuild in Kensington. This included highly decorative, burnished silver lifts, thrilling to enter and shoot up to the roof gardens.

Lifts required attendants. To the regret of many a male customer, Selfridges' smart young women were replaced after the Second World War by disabled ex-servicemen. In 1970 these decadent elevators were swapped for more modern escalators. Other stores resisted change. When Charles Digby Harrod capitulated and finally

Walter Gilbert's bronze Art Deco elevator screen for Derry & Toms, 1933 (sold at auction in 2019 for $20,000).

installed six opulent, brass and marble Otis lifts in the Edwardian era, they were there to stay. You can ride them still.

BEARMANS
829–837 High Road, Leytonstone, E11 • 1898–1983

Bearmans – the 'Harrods of East London' – took Christmas out of the store and into the street. Father Christmas arrived in twentieth-century Leytonstone by sleigh (and later gondola, submarine, even space rocket), travelling along the High Road with his reindeer on a float flanked by penguins, dancing girls and elves. High-wattage lights fizzed and flickered,

crowds cheered, children gaped. Father Christmas (*never* 'Santa') was on his way to Bearmans' Toy Fair.

Upstairs at the store, the magic continued. The North Pole was hidden in a cavern full of elves and fairies; children had to take special mechanised transport to get there. Anthony Elliot, who worked at Bearmans from 1962 to 1975, remembers Father Christmas receiving guests from a speedboat one year, with children approaching past an ornamental pond full of battery-operated fish and a fountain. This was the year Father Christmas made a fatal error of timing.

When the grand doors to his grotto opened and an eager crowd of children pressed forward, he was seen, 'in all his glory, having a quick tinkle in the fountain'. He was sacked on the spot and a replacement hastily found.

'The Store with the Personal Touch' was opened by young draper Frank Bearman in 1898, when Leytonstone was little more than a village. The gamble paid off: it was to remain a thriving family business for the next 64 years. Frank and Kate Bearman were the couple who brought the West End shopping experience to Leytonstone, adding a beautiful arcade in 1910 in direct imitation of central London's finest. Why go into town when you had Bearmans on your doorstep?

Post-war, an extension was added in Kirkdale Road with an escalator – the first one outside central London.

By the 60s Bearmans had 450 employees; many still reminisce about their jobs with loyal affection. 'Best days of my young life', remembers Julie Bocock, who did her hairdressing apprenticeship in the Bearmans salon. The store moved with the times, opening the Melody Bar for Music ('Audition rooms! Record of the Week corner! Individual Listening!'), but Frank's sons didn't share their father's passion for retail. In 1962 they sold up to the London Co-operative

Society. After the store's closure in 1983, the building was demolished. A Matalan now stands on the spot.

One Sunday night in January 1958, a gang of masked raiders broke into the store with the aim of stealing the weekend's takings of £15,000. Using three sticks of gelignite, they blew down the doors to the strong room, but couldn't manage to break into the safe itself. They fled with just a handful of watches after smashing open a display case. The night watchman, 'Big Jim' Milne, was bound, gagged and blindfolded but managed to free himself with a penknife.

BODGERS 113 High Road, Ilford, IG1 • 1890-2018

Bodgers' famous sales were irresistible. They would draw, 'like a magnet, thousands of bargain hunters from all parts of London and Essex', reported the *Eastern Counties Times* in 1930. Such was the crush at one sale that a large, plate-glass shop window gave way. 'Eager customers streamed into the shop through the jagged opening.'

This was 'Ilford's favourite discount store', 'the Store of the Thrifty'. As its advertisements went, there were 'Bargains Galore at the John Bodger Store'.

Over 7,000 queued for the Bodgers closing-down sale, 2017.

When John Adams Guy Bodger died in 1920, aged 74, he was a household name in Ilford. He'd been a Justice of the Peace, a local and county councillor and an eminent local Freemason, as well as a successful department store owner with prodigious energy and clear empathy for his fellow workers. He was a leading figure in the Early Closing Association, chairing their annual meeting in 1915. The Association's aim was to get shops to close at 8 p.m. three nights a week, at 9 p.m. on Fridays and at 10 p.m. on Saturdays. In March 1915, 17 London department stores agreed

to close at 8 p.m. three nights a week: a victory for Bodger and his allies.

Bargains ran in Bodger's blood. When he and his wife

Juliet took over an old drapery store at 113 High Road in 1890, they threw open their doors at 7 p.m. with a clearance sale.

And so began the expansion of 'John Bodger Ilford Drapery Emporium' – first into neighbouring premises on Ilford High Road and Station Road, then opening the Bodger's Station Arcade in 1914, famous for its daily demonstrations of mechanical toys in the run-up to Christmas.

The department store kept pace with the craze for stunts and demonstrations, hiring (for example) the services of Madame Amie Stobbs, 'The World Renowned Anatomist and Speciality Fitter', in 1913 to enhance the store's Imperial Cygnia Corsets exhibition. 'Why not take advantage of the inestimable benefits she can confer on you?' ran the adverts. 'She will achieve results in figure culture which will be a revelation to you.'

By 1930, with a Modernist rebuild behind them,

the store was simply 'Bodgers': employing 300, with sleeping and dining accommodation available on Ilford High Road. John's son Frank shared his father's concern for his fellow workers' welfare.

Bodgers was taken over by the Morleys Stores Group in 1959, added to in the 70s and 80s, and still a household word in Ilford for excellent service and unbeatable prices. But it couldn't compete with the Westfield Stratford City shopping centre, which opened in 2011. Bodgers closed its doors in 2018.

Planning application for a massive, 42-storey 'Bodgers Tower' met with fierce resistance from locals, but was passed by Redbridge Council in 2019. The project has since been delayed by arguments over the proportion of affordable housing.

HARRISON GIBSON
193–207 High Road, Ilford, IG1 • 1902–2010

On Tuesday, 17 March 1959, Ilford's residents woke to a smouldering town centre. The 'biggest fire since the Blitz!' (according to Pathé News) had been brought under control by 250 firemen. 'Not since the big raids of the war has anything like it been known in England.' The High Road's famous home furnishings store lay in embers, along with 12 smaller shops and Moulton's drapery store. All day, cars queued to see the burnt-out shell of Ilford High Road.

'I went by the shop the morning after,' remembers Brian Watson, 'just to gawp, and there was a rather sad little ladies' hat on a display spike in what was left of the window, still smoking.' Also watching the smoke rise was the phlegmatic John C. Gibson, known as 'Mr John' to his 350 staff. 'We shall rebuild,' he vowed. 'I have seen this before. We were burned down here before in 1924.'

It was true: 'Mr John' had twice been through trial by fire. Two months after the death of his Yorkshire-

born father, store founder John Harrison Gibson, an electrical fault burst into flame at 8 a.m. The blaze quickly took hold, tearing through this 'complete house furnishers' department store full of wooden furniture and

bedding. 'Mr John' was seen pacing up and down with a walking stick (a war veteran, he'd lost a leg in the Somme), watching as his business went up in flames. A brand-new building replaced it within a year, topped with two roof garden restaurants, 'as luxurious as anything in London, New York and Paris.'

For the same thing to happen 25 years later was incredible. It was reported in 1959 that the lock-up man had smelt petrol the night before; there were suspicions of arson, 'someone with a grudge'. Either way, less than 48 hours after the flames were doused, drawings of the new store were in circulation.

Staff remember letting balloons off from the roof of the new, 11-storey Harrison Gibson building when it reopened, overseen by John ('Jack') G. Gibson, ebullient grandson of the founder. 'Morning, Mr Gibson,' they'd say, lining up as their boss arrived by chauffeur-driven Bentley or, on occasion, a Ford Thunderbird.

The range of products was extraordinary, beautifully made, and of enduring quality – from Chinese rugs to

'The biggest blaze in this town's history' – *Ilford Recorder*, 1959. Was it arson? Two days after the flames were doused, drawings of the new store were in circulation.

Indian furniture, leather suites to contemporary art. Modern touches included basement parking, a crèche and an interior design department. On top of all this – quite literally – sat the Chariot restaurant and the Room at the Top nightclub.

Harrison Gibson – 'HG' – is remembered fondly by those who grew up in Ilford in the 60s and 70s, an era when the town's high street was the envy of Essex. The company also had stores in Bromley, Bedford, Doncaster, Manchester, Leeds and Halifax. By another cruel twist of fate, Bromley's Harrison Gibson also burned down, in 1968 (sold that same year to the Army & Navy group, closed in 2004).

When the nearby Stratford Centre opened in 1974, Ilford's 'HG' took a hit. Acquired first by Harveys' furniture chain, its slide down-market ended with closure in 2010. A 30-storey, 330-home tower block is now planned for the site, in an attempt to reinvigorate the 'wasteland' of Ilford's High Road.

J. R. ROBERTS   78–102 Broadway, Stratford, E15 • 1870–1975

After weeks of secret preparation, on Monday, 3 December 1888, the heavy mahogany doors of J. R. Roberts opened onto a cavernous, twinkling fairytale. For one enchanted month, children could step away from the noise and chill of Broadway and enter a world of unimaginable fantasy. This was the first Santa's Grotto to open in a London department store.

Some 17,000 children visited Roberts' Grotto during Christmas 1888, each accompanied by an adult paying one penny. It was an inspired method of fund-raising. John Reynolds Roberts was by now a wealthy man, a Camberwell-born, working-class philanthropist who chose to donate the proceeds to West Ham Hospital (later Queen Mary's Hospital for the East End). Yet he was, at heart,

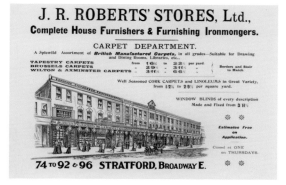

a merchant. Having ensnared this new, captive audience, Roberts was going to shift as many toys as he possibly could.

'Marvelous collections of Cheap Toys, New Games, Dolls, Puzzles, Engines in Motion, Tops, Horse and Carts, Tram Cars, Rocking Horses, Swings, Jumping Dogs and Cats, Clown and Pig, and other Animal Toys', proclaimed the advertisements in the local press,

conjuring a vanished world of Victorian ingenuity, craftsmanship and humour, such as the anarchic clown astride a pig.

Stratford's Santa's Grotto was imitated throughout London's big stores the following Christmas. When Roberts sold his business six years later, aged 60, the festive tradition had become a cherished part of the department store's identity. By 1910, East End children could find a 'wonderfully realistic' miniature theatre putting on productions of Cinderella and Red Riding Hood, where 'ingenious mechanical figures' acted out the familiar fairytales against a real waterfall and mill,

with real goldfish swimming in a real river. Inside a real cottage was a bed; in the bed, was the Wolf. Real or mechanical, it was hard to tell.

J. R. Roberts was sold to the London Co-operative Society in 1950, and then four years later acquired by Hide & Co of Kingston on Thames, which was in turn was absorbed into House of Fraser in 1975. The original store buildings were demolished (to much local consternation) and rebuilt by the London Co-operative Society between 1957 and 1962. The premises have since been occupied by Dixon's/Curry's, Morrison's Local, and now a pub.

WICKHAMS 69–89 Mile End Road, Whitechapel, E1 • 1850s–1969

Once seen, never forgotten. Wickhams of Mile End Road is, as the architectural critic Ian Nairn put it in 1966, 'one of London's best visual jokes'. Halfway along the grandiose, colonnaded front, about as subtle as a missing tooth, is a small, two-storey Victorian shop. This is a satisfying tale of David and Goliath; of East End pluck and indomitability in the face of big business.

The Wickham family had started humbly enough in the 1850s as drapers on Mile End Road, expanding

sideways bit by bit, taking over other shops. By the 1920s they had bigger ambitions. They wanted a store to rival Selfridges, the sort of department store that was now transforming London's high streets, pushing out small businesses and aggressively eating up competing trade. The architects T. Jay Evans and Son were commissioned, borrowing for their design Selfridges' Ionic columns and adding an imposing central clock tower.

The remaining shops were bought up, clearing the way for the massive rebuild. With one exception. Wickhams met its match in Spiegelhalters. This flourishing little clockmaker and jewellers had already been bumped out of number 75 in 1892 to accommodate an earlier Wickhams expansion. The German family had been in business in Whitechapel since 1828. Otto Spiegelhalter and his brothers would not be moving again, whatever the offer. It's said that Wickhams' lawyers promised to cover the shop floor with gold sovereigns to get the family out. The Spielgelhalters responded that they'd consider it – but only if the coins were stood on edge.

A compromise was reached. The Spiegelhalters sold their back garden to Wickhams, so the store could build behind them. In 1925, with the proceeds, they installed

A spanner in the works: jeweller and clockmaker Spiegelhalter.

a beautiful Deco shopfront, all curved glass and sinuous lettering. Wickhams, meanwhile, ended up an off-kilter, gap-toothed department store, finished in 1927. The illuminated tower was off-centre: seven window bays on one side, nine on the other. The emporium was later remembered as 'lacking in "dazzle"', even if it did have a tennis court on its roof.

Spiegelhalters had the last laugh. While Wickhams closed in 1969, the clockmaker and jewellers ran their business on Mile End Road until 1988, when they sold up to an off-licence and relocated to Essex. The name is still trading today from Penzance. By 2014 the tiny shop was derelict and roofless, yet when developers unveiled plans to turn the former department store into a trendy Whitechapel office block, locals mounted a fierce campaign to keep this cherished symbol of the little man's triumph. Not only had it become a local landmark, it had also crept into East End argot. To 'Spiegelhalt' someone is to put a spanner in the works.

Department W, repurposed by Buckley Gray Yeoman, is a 'blank canvas': a workspace-led, mixed-use development stripped back to original features. Pleasingly, the old Spielgelhalters façade forms the main entrance: 'the heart and soul of the building rather than the thorn in its side', claim the architects, whose project was shortlisted for the RIBA Awards in 2022. At ground level are a Tesco Express and a Sports Direct.

JEREMIAH ROTHERHAM & CO — 76–91 Shoreditch High Street, E1 • 1840–1968

One cold, November day in 1891, a barrister named Montagu Williams, on a mercy mission to buy blankets and petticoats for the poor, took a hansom cab to Jeremiah Rotherham & Co on Shoreditch High Street. Williams wrote up his impressions, and to read them is to be propelled, dizzyingly, through one of those great department stores at their High Victorian zenith.

'At Messrs Rotherham's you see one department stacked with carpets; another, with merinos and dress goods; a third, with rich and beautiful silks; a fourth – resembling a gigantic and well stocked conservatory – with artificial flowers, the pick of the Paris and London markets; a fifth, with thousands of rolls of ribbons, representing every colour known to the dyer; a sixth, with great heaps of straw hats . . . '

Williams had asked one of the partners what all

this stock was worth. 'Something not far short of £200,000,' came the reply.

This vast store was one of the sights of the City: an adventure to be written up in much the same way Victorian journalists visited the slums. Rotherham's backed up against the worst of Shoreditch, and the stark contrast with the 'infamous' Boundary Street area added to the frisson. As he left, Williams noticed the scrupulously clean stables next door servicing a fleet of delivery carriages. Each stall bore a nameplate: Jess, Dolly, Punch, Vic, Spot. 'Would that human beings living hard by were as comfortably housed as those horses!'

Jeremiah Rotherham was a Derbyshire man who lost his wife Sophia in the East End cholera epidemic of 1849. At 51, she was ten years his senior. Having no children, he chose four long-term employees from the shop floor as partners; 'warehousemen' who dedicated their working lives (71 years, in one case) to making the business a success.

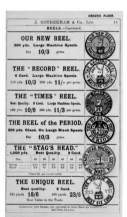
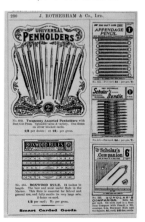

They served him well. The empire prospered, but it didn't escape the Blitz. An enemy bomb destroyed the main building on Shoreditch High Street in 1941. Business transferred to a new warehouse, and by 1958 was facing liquidation.

Jeremiah Rotherham's had never before appointed external directors. That was not the way they did things. But in such dire straits, the aged directors were forcibly retired and a wealthy Anglo-Iraqi ushered in to shore up the company.

Nadji Khazam and his sister, Flora Yentob, had controlling interests in a number of Manchester textile companies – and, eventually, a connection with another great British institution. Flora Yentob's son, Alan Yentob, became Creative Director at the BBC. Rotherham's, meanwhile, became a pawn in a more global retail game. After a series of takeovers and mergers, Jeremiah Rotherham & Co – or at least its assets – was absorbed into a larger company in 1968.

Fashion retailing has returned to the site, a new 2019 building housing a 5,000-square-foot store for the Swedish denim brand Weekday.

The Invention of Christmas

It all started in 1888 with J. R. Roberts of Stratford, the first in London to create a Christmas Grotto with a real, live Santa Claus (see page 94). Seventeen thousand children visited. By 1889, it was already rare for a

department store not to offer a Christmas experience. Even the no-nonsense Army & Navy pulled together a 'gargantuan display' of bon-bons, bugles, hoops and

Only 39 shopping days to Christmas!
Christmas arrived early for Quin & Axtens in 1927, with Santa Claus parading through Brixton in a coach drawn by four grey horses, 'replete with coachman, guard and horn blower', before climbing in through a first-floor window. It was 10 November: the church calendar had been pushed aside – now department stores announced the festive season earlier and earlier. Harry Gordon Selfridge led the hype, coming up with the slogan 'Only XX shopping days to Christmas'.

china dolls. Shoolbred's Christmas Toy Bazaar, allegedly 'the finest in London', soon became a major attraction.

Gorringes claimed to be 'alone in having a floor devoted exclusively to presents'. Bentalls of Kingston went on to have its own circus, complete with elephant and lion (kept overnight in the lift shaft). Shop windows exerted such a magnetic pull at Christmas that in 1909 the police had to be called to Swan & Edgar because the weight of people at the windows on the corner of Great Marlborough Street and Regent Street had entirely blocked the road, bringing the traffic to a standstill.

Santa at Shinners, Sutton: Caroline and Lucille Morris, 1959.

Gamages' famous Christmas Bazaar outdid them all with 'the Greatest Exhibition of Toys in London. Over Four Acres of Floor Space, A Veritable Emporium of Delight. Great Show Pieces! See the Embarkation of the

Father Christmas arrives early at Arding & Hobbs, Clapham Junction: it's 2 November 1926.

'A Vortex of Would-Be Buyers'

'In Swan and Edgar's this morning, the hubbub on the staircase was simply deafening. A continual stream of "sightseers" wended their way up and down . . . I leave D.H. Evans and retrace my steps as far as Oxford Circus. The windows in Peter Robinson's are so enthralling it seems a pity to go in . . . I stand for a moment at Marshall & Snelgrove's window, and my feminine heart begins to pine for the beauties behind the glass.'

The Outlook, 1898

Army Corps! Hall of Mystery! Conjuring Entertainment!'

By the mid-1920s, inspired by great American stores such as Macy's, imaginations were running riot. At Chiesmans in Lewisham, Santa's Grotto in 1927 was a 'wonderful jungle and farmyard cave' with automated lions roaring, monkeys climbing trees, and Little Red Riding Hood at home. Next year saw the 'Great Polar Bear Cave with polar bears, Eskimos, seals and penguins, all electrically controlled and emitting the sounds peculiar to their kind'.

THE ROYAL ARSENAL CO-OPERATIVE SOCIETY (RACS)

Powis Street, SE18 and Lewisham High Street, SE13 • 1868-1985

Unlike the more middle-class Army & Navy, the RACS was a service to the working classes. 'Each for All and All for Each' was the motto emblazoned over its door (you can see this still today, on Powis Street).

South London's antidote to rampant capitalism was founded on enlightened, democratic principles: one member, one vote, with profit shared among all. By 1889 it was the largest co-operative society in the capital; social reformer Charles Booth thought there was 'nothing at all like it within the boundaries of London'.

It had its own education department. It ran classes and sports days, a cricket club and two orchestras. By the 1930s the RACS had two choirs conducted by (Sir) Michael Tippett. The society opened its first free lending library in Woolwich in 1879, some 20 years before the local authority provided one. Right from the beginning, it was decided that 2.5 per cent of profits should be spent on education. By 1975, with half a million members and a reach as far as the Home Counties, those profits were considerable.

The enterprise was started in 1868 by Woolwich Royal Arsenal munitions workers William Rose and

Alexander Macleod, who corralled 20 fellow workers to pay a £1 share, then hosted the first sale of tea, 100lb of sugar and two crocks of butter. Five years later they expanded into shop premises in Powis Street. By 1877, with an 8hp engine and dough-kneading machinery, the society produced (as their precise accounts showed) 476,027 4lb loaves – delivered by 11 horse-drawn vans to members, known as 'co-operators'.

The RACS's ambition and expansion have left behind

Business is conducted in the third-floor restaurant of the Moderne Woolwich store, 1963.

The ground floor 'economy department' sold cheaper, smaller goods – shown here after the 1964 refit.

a series of landmark buildings in and around London, including those at its beating heart, Powis Street in Woolwich. The red-brick and terracotta Edwardian headquarters was built here, 1903–26, in imitation of Harrods. Opposite is the startlingly different Art Deco department store, opened in 1940, its streamlined horizontal lines influenced by Joseph Emberton's Simpson's of Piccadilly (1935–6). The building's cream faience tiles were made by the Leeds Fireclay Company, while the aluminium Crittall windows came from the same company who'd kitted out the *Titanic* and New York's Tudor City apartments. The wrought-iron railings of the tallest tower's stairwell spelled out 'CO-OP' in Modernist curves. The RACS might serve the working man and woman, but it had architectural aspiration and panache in spades.

The Lewisham 'Tower House' RACS department store drew thousands at its High Street opening in 1933: an attention-grabbing, red-brick and marble Art Deco façade with little ships, trains and lorries in jaunty bas relief. As dusk fell, the neon letters 'RACS' and '1868–1933' glowed from its central tower.

But the Society wasn't just about department stores. It reached its paternalistic tentacles into every branch of life – and death. Services included removals, catering, laundry, insurance, savings clubs and undertakers; there were bookshops, jewellers, shoe shops, hairdressers and chemists. To support its retail activities, the RACS established bakeries, bought farms and piggeries, built food-processing factories. It owned stables and railway wagons, an abattoir, dairy, a frozen food plant, a fleet of coaches and two hotels on the Isle of Wight.

Unusually for a co-operative, the RACS affiliated itself with the Labour Party, supporting the landslide 1902 election of trade unionist Will Crooks as MP for Woolwich. In the Fifties, it sponsored a series of candidates for south-east London, many of whom were successful.

The Society reached its zenith in 1975 – but just as membership topped half a million, shopping habits began to change, and fast. Greater affluence, together with the rise of the supermarket chains, saw RACS's loyal 'co-operators' decline drastically. In 1985, after a century of expansion, it was absorbed into the national Co-operative Wholesale Society. The modernist department store on Powis Street, which finally closed its doors in 1999, later enjoyed a moment of notoriety when its desolate, abandoned interior was used for the 2007 dystopian science fiction film, *Children of Men*.

All you could need: the travel department, and (left) bar.

Saved from demolition, the Deco RACS building has been converted into luxury flats.

The abandoned interior was used as a dystopian film set in 2007.

In 2011–13 the red-brick Edwardian headquarters was converted into a 120-room hotel, operating today as Woolwich Travelodge.

Threatened with demolition by Greenwich Council, the Deco store opposite was happily saved and converted, in 2013–16, into Emporium SE18 – 58 apartments and penthouses for 'luxury living in the heart of Woolwich'. Tower House on Lewisham High Street today houses apartments, office space, retail units and a gym.

CHIESMANS
33–61 High Street, Lewisham, SE13 • 1884–1997

In April 1932, Lewisham's shoppers were titillated to discover a lion in residence at the High Street's favourite department store. They took this in their stride. 'Vixen, the untamed lioness' was just the latest in a series of animal circus stunts intended to pull in the crowds. In 1930 Chiesmans had welcomed to its basement a 'veritable zoo' – 'a Noah's Ark of hundreds of living birds and animals and reptiles' direct from the Ideal Home Exhibition at Olympia. In 1931, the three Chiesman brothers added ponies, elephants and snakes. Vixen the lioness arrived next, courtesy of Chipperfield's.

'See the young English trainer enter the den of the untameable lion!' promised the advertisement. No

Chiesmans' staff were loyal: many joined straight from school and worked to retirement. In 1938, a Miss Roberts (ribbon buyer) and Mr Coleman (maintenance manager) were presented with 'substantial cheques' to mark 50 years with the company, noted the *Norwood News*; there

was also a Mr Brewitt who had been there since 1901. In 1964 it was announced that the Chiesman stores would be opening for longer, but their 230 Lewisham staff would work fewer hours – 4.5 rather than 5.5 days per week – for the same pay.

matter that Vixen was a famously sleepy lioness – it was all part of the Chiesman art of showmanship. Promotion ran in their blood. Even the disastrous flooding of Lewisham High Street in 1968, above, was turned to advantage, with Chiesmans announcing a 'Gigantic Flood Sale' of its damaged basement stock.

When Victorian founders Frank and Harry Chiesman took over Paris House, an established draper's store on 15 Lewisham High Street in 1884, they had already trained with the best. Frank had worked at Gorringes in Buckingham Palace Road, Harry at Whiteleys in Bayswater, while both had spent time working in the *grands magasins* of Paris. Into the mix came Florence Waterhouse, one of the first assistants in the brothers' drapery, proposed to by Harry Chiesman. Together,

relentlessly, the family expanded the business, always looking out for novel ways to attract customers – and especially at Christmas.

By 1911, Chiesmans claimed to be 'The most convenient, commodious, comfortable and economical shopping centre In Kent'. By 1926, it was 'Kent's premier shopping rendezvous'. Chiesmans would become the largest department store in south-east London, with a network of branches from Essex to the Isle of Wight. When founders Frank and Harry died in 1938 and 1940, the brand was already safe in the hands of their sons Stuart, Russell and Howard.

Many stunts, sales and promotions later (including electrically controlled Eskimos, an Easter Egg Farm with live hens, and the arrival of MGM's film star Marcus the Gladiator in a horse-drawn chariot), Chiesmans Ltd was acquired by House of Fraser in 1976 and eventually rebranded Army & Navy. The flagship store in Lewisham finally closed in 1997.

> In 2001 the store was demolished, to be replaced by Lewisham Police Station – one of the biggest purpose-built stations in Europe, with the largest custody suite in the Metropolitan Police. It still has a bridge across Granville Grove, and fits neatly into the old Chiesmans footprint – including stabling for 36 police horses.

HOLDRONS 135 Rye Lane, Peckham, SE15 • 1882-1949

Opposite Peckham Rye's ornate Victorian station sits a monolithic, maltreated yet cherished institution of SE15: Khan's Bargains. Stacks of boxes crowd its

windows. The tiled façade, coated in butterscotch paint, is chipped and grimy. Garish plastic wares clutter up the pavement. It takes a leap of imagination (and perhaps some insider knowledge) to see that this is, in fact, a jewel of 1930s department store architecture.

'I love this building,' cries Peckham architect, Benedict O'Looney. 'It's so strong and forceful, with its huge Modernist swathes of metal and glass.' Designed in the early 1930s by T. P. Bennett, it was originally clad in a glazed terracotta façade with shimmering white-cream tiles – the perfect wipe-clean material for a London store front.

Khan's was once Holdrons – 'The shop that made Peckham famous,' the pride of Rye Lane's Golden Mile. This was the store where Thirties film star Molly Lamont opened an exhibition of chinaware; where

children flocked to see the largest model railway display in Europe; where daily mannequin parades filled the thousand-seater fashion hall decorated in 'black and white with splashes of magenta'.

Step inside and, above the boxes of savoury crackers and jars of pickled lemons, you'll find a tantalising glimpse of the past. In 2019, the false ceilings were ripped out to reveal a spectacular Art Deco vaulted light well made of 'Lenscrete': one thousand glass lenses set in a concrete and steel grid. Outside again, look up at the store front once more and admire the fluted Art Deco detailing recently discovered behind the giant blue plastic sign advertising Mr Khan's bargains.

Draper Harry Holdron appreciated a bargain. 'Big Price Reductions' and 'Household Bargain Week' were his advertising stock in trade. The business started in an unpretentious, single-story block at 117–125 Rye Lane

in 1882; a decade later, he'd expanded either side and earned a reputation for long opening hours, frequent sales and special reductions.

An Edwardian rebuild followed in Flemish brick, giving Mr Holdron a handsome, Harrods-esque building together with a fashionable 'Parisian passage' with vaulted glazed glass roof, in imitation of the West End's Burlington Arcade.

In 1926 Holdrons was snapped up by Selfridges, and the Jazz Age burst into the store with all-day Charleston dance-offs in

the elegant restaurant. When the ambitious Thirties rebuild was commissioned, Peckham's citizens were asked to vote for their favourite from a design shortlist – Neo-Georgian, Beaux Arts and Modernist. Perhaps surprisingly, they rejected tradition for an ostentatious Moderne statement. The architect (who at that time was working on John Barnes of Finchley) sketched out a store three times bigger than was eventually built.

By the time the doors swung open in September 1935, local interest was intense. 'Exhilarating to look at in its clean, modernistic beauty,' pronounced the *South London Press* – 'the store has been so designed throughout to have an almost irresistible appeal.' *Almost irresistible* . . . As Zola had written half a century earlier, 'just get the women, and you will sell the world!' Holdrons specifically targeted women, promoting hard its vast new fashion floor, seducing with the lure of the brand new: 'The Stock! The Fittings! The Atmosphere! New Authentic Fashions at the Low Prices you always expect at Holdrons!'

It's apt that Holdrons has today been reinvented as a different kind of 'Store of the People' (as Khan's tote bags proudly proclaim, using the original store's slogan). For the first half of the twentieth century, Holdrons ('For Value') sat at the heart of Peckham's community. Acquired by the John Lewis Partnership in 1940, it was sold on in 1949 to an investment company: a bitter blow. One thousand staff lost their jobs, and the building began an inexorable decline. The Times Furnishing Company moved in, followed eventually by Blockbuster Video – when those glinting faience tiles were painted Blockbuster blue.

Khan's Bargains is, to some, the jewel in Peckham's crown. Akbar Khan first came to the UK from Afghanistan in 1999, where his family ran a retail business in Kabul. After arriving in London with little spoken English, he started trading on a Rye Lane market stall, opening Khan's Bargains a year later.

Mr Khan is on a mission to help get more traders involved in preserving Peckham's architectural

heritage. 'I would encourage other shopkeepers to visit my shop and see that behind more recent coverings, there are often beautiful historic features to be discovered and restored,' he says. 'My shop is now a much brighter and more beautiful place to visit. This restoration work has helped my business and has been exciting to do.'

Khan intends to continue the restoration process begun in 2019 with the encouragement of local conservation architect Benedict O'Looney. Together with two local handymen known as Tony and Pops, they are all peeling back the layers to reveal the building's original robust and beautiful features. Work has begun on removing the thick yellow paint from the faience tiles, and fixing the Art Deco windows. A renaissance is taking place on Rye Lane.

JONES & HIGGINS
1 Rye Lane, Peckham, SE15 • 1867–1980

Competing for Peckham's shoppers at the other end of Rye Lane's 'Golden Mile' was Jones & Higgins, with its Venetian clock tower and stupendous, stampeding sales. 'What a dreary aspect this little southern suburb has,' wrote Edwin Jones back in 1867, on visiting his Peckham-based brother. Dreary – but fast growing. He noticed that the only draper's shop was doing brisk business, and he smelt opportunity.

By March that year, young drapers' apprentices Edwin Jones and George Randell Higgins had opened a shop at 1 Rye Lane, on the corner of Peckham High Street. And as the village got swallowed up by the metropolis and its 'genteel villas', so they flourished, by 1888 occupying the entire block. By the 1890s Peckham was noted as 'a great shopping centre' with Jones & Higgins at its core, 'which crowds buzz around all day'. The *South London Press* published a flattering profile

of the mighty store in its Victorian heyday – beginning with an account of the 'exceptional, even phenomenal' annual sale, 'so inconveniently crowded within half an hour that the firm was compelled to close the door and let the public in by batches at intervals. The sale causes so many heart flutters in so many feminine bosoms.'

Mindful of Holdron's nearby expansion, Mr Jones and Mr Higgins schemed to put down a visual marker: an architectural flourish to signal their superiority. They engaged leading Southwark architects Henry Jarvis & Sons (responsible for Dulwich Hospital), who hit upon bringing a bit of Venice, no less, to Peckham.

The famous clock tower was built in 1893, the crowning glory of the store's elegant expansion. Sitting at the nucleus of Peckham village, the landmark tower took its inspiration from the Renaissance Torre

Del'Orologio of St Mark's Square in Venice. It was a bold investment, and it paid off. Shoppers flocked.

In 1914, Charles Higgins placed the firm's male hostel at the disposal of the War Office. One year later, Hanover Lodge became the 35-bed Hanover Park VAD Hospital, an auxiliary to the First London (TF) General Hospital in Cormont Road, Camberwell. Increased to 50 beds in May 1917, it was staffed by three trained nurses and 90 part-time VADs.

In 1908 Holdrons hit back with its fashionable shopping arcade – but, in the end, Jones & Higgins outlived its competitor by some 30 years, reinventing itself to stay relevant. A 1960s boutique, 'Jones Girl', opened, along with a record department, launched by DJ Tony Blackburn – a popular haunt for many Peckham teenagers idling away their lunch hours and Saturday afternoons. The store closed in 1980, but J&H anecdotes still swirl around Peckham to this day, part of its rich local mythology. Anyone remember 'Ferny'

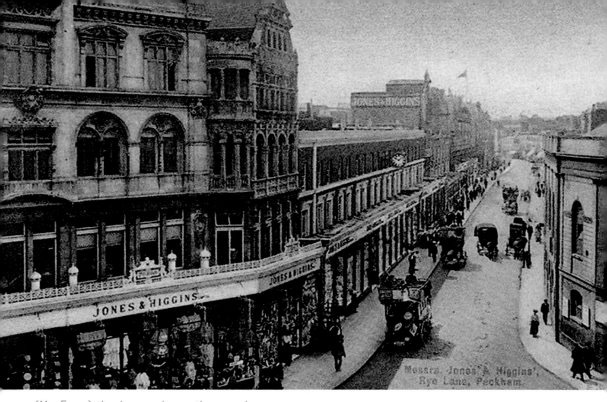

Messrs. Jones & Higgins,
Rye Lane, Peckham.

(Mrs Fearn), the dragon who ran the record department? Or Morris, the talking mynah bird? Then there's the story of the Santa Claus stuck overnight in the lift in '68, or the South American honey bear found in the 'bargain box' of men's ties . . .

> 'I used to cause mayhem running around all the departments in Jones & Higgins. The staff were so friendly back then.' – *Tony Haycock*
> 'Does anyone remember the secret staircase to get to the carpet department?' – *Sue Welling*

Part of the building was demolished to make room for the Aylesham Centre shopping mall; the rest, surmounted by the famous clocktower, got taken over by the Peckham Palais nightclub, a beloved, infamous venue oozing 'raw charm' with capacity for 1,500 clubbers. Today, without an occupier or purpose, the grandest building in Peckham is falling into ruin. Griff Rhys Jones (of the Victorian Society) is campaigning for its restoration as a 'valuable heritage asset'.

Audacious Women

Hilda Harvey

The pinnacle of Hilda Harvey's career came at the early age of 32. As Staff Controller at Selfridges, Women's Division, she was responsible for engaging and supervising a staff of over 3,000 women and girls. The year was 1917: she was the first woman to hold such a senior position at a London department store.

Hilda joined Selfridges aged 23 as a short-hand typist in 1909, a month

before the great store opened for business. The timing could not have been better. Harry Gordon Selfridge believed in employing and promoting women; he was, after all, courting female customers. Hilda became private secretary to one of the directors, then secretary of the staff record bureau, climbing to the top job during the Great War. A founder member of the Soroptomists Club and a staunch promoter of women's interests, Hilda married in 1913 and became Mrs Funnell. At Selfridges, however, she was always known as 'Miss Harvey'.

Alice Diamond and the Forty Elephants

Outwardly respectable in her cloche hat and furs, Alice Diamond was one of the most brazen thieves known to department store detectives – indeed, to Scotland Yard. From 1915 to her death in 1952 she ran a ring of female shoplifters known as the Forty Thieves, or even the Forty Elephants, as they hailed from the Elephant and Castle in south London.

These women could walk into a store and 'literally strip it': Debenham & Freebody, D. H. Evans, Selfridges, Whiteleys . . . One would create a distraction – pretend

to faint, or ask to examine an item in the daylight – leaving the others to shove furs, silks, jewellery and leather goods down voluminous bloomers elasticated at the knee. The Queen, Alice Diamond (pictured top left), would sell on everything they stole via a network of local fences, paying her gang members generous wages. During the 1940s 'hoisters' might earn a hundred pounds a week, out-earning men's average wages ten-to-one.

'Queen Alice' had been born in Lambeth Workhouse but travelled by chauffeur-driven Chrysler and was known for her stylish dress ('putting on the posh'), wild partying and knuckleduster diamond rings.

A Wave of Naked Greed and Animality

On the stroke of 9 a.m. a woman draws back the bolts and ceremoniously opens the doors. The crowd pours in as though a dam is breaking – a wave of naked greed and animality. It is mayhem. Umbrella tips and toe caps are used, even hat pins. A woman screams. There is a tussle over French lace; the store manager is called. *This* is the ultra-civilised Peter Robinson in the Victorian year of 1897.

Sales fever was – still is? – a peculiarly female affliction. Twice a year, women would find themselves in the grip of obsessive, transporting behaviour, acting against all their normal instincts. How did this all start?

In 1878 the first 'White Sale' was held by the American department store entrepreneur John Wanamaker of Philadelphia, in an attempt to shift stock after Christmas. He came up with the cynical sales pitch of a 'clean start' for the New Year – and his surplus white linen flew out of the store. And so, twice a year, with the men holding the strings, female consumers were made to dance like helpless marionettes, regardless of class or pocket. Who could resist a bargain, or a stab at upward mobility? The Winter Sale, in particular, remains the greatest moment of madness in the consumer calendar.

While some sales were civilised (Swears & Wells customers got served refreshments as they queued),

Debenhams, 1977 – and 'sales fever' is no longer confined to women.

behaviour became increasingly feral. At Bodgers in Ilford in the late 1920s, crowds burst through a plate glass window. Pathé footage of Selfridges' sale, 1957, shows middle-aged women in hats and pebble glasses burrowing through candlewick bedspreads like frenzied dogs, culminating in a vicious tug of war. At Harrods in 1981 ('There Is Only One Sale'), 400 people fought their way into the electricals department for a 26' Dynatron Remote Control TV at half price. In the melée, a woman fell and split her head, and the sales manager was roughed up. This time, almost all the shoppers were male.

'No, no, I'm not going in,' Madame de Boves muttered. 'I'm afraid. Come on, Blanche, let's go, we'll be crushed.'

But her voice was growing weaker and gradually she gave in to the desire to follow everyone inside, her fears dissolving in the irresistible attraction of the crush. Madame Marty, too, had ceased to resist. She kept saying: 'Hold my dress, Valentine. Well, I never! I've never seen such a thing! What can it be like inside!' ...

A nursemaid, right in the thick of it, lifted her baby above her head while it laughed happily. And just one scrawny woman was losing her temper, pouring out a string of abuse, accusing the lady next to her of elbowing her.

'I really think they'll have the skirt off me,' Madame de Boves kept saying.'

Emile Zola, *Au Bonheur Des Dames (The Ladies' Delight)*, 1883

ALLDERS  2 North End, Croydon, CR0 • 1862-2012

By 2000, Allders of Croydon was the third largest department store in Britain after Harrods and Selfridges, and the flagship of a chain of 45. In its final century, the brand grew ever larger and ever more distant from its essentially modest founder. Its nineteenth-century story revolves around the benign force of one individual.

Draper's assistant Joshua Allder left Southwark for Croydon in 1862, with his pregnant wife Jane and

one-year-old Alice. He was an energetic 24-year-old, Croydon a growing town; he opened a drapers' shop at 102–3 North End and put his back into it. Soon the shop had expanded into 104, 106 and 107 North End, though they had to wait for some 20 years to acquire

105, a tenacious little bakery.

A photograph taken in the late 1880s shows a middle-aged Joshua with long, grizzled beard and a sprightly-looking wife, surrounded by some 50 staff. He sits just off centre, resting his arm in his wife's lap. Their staff are lean-faced, young, smartly dressed, closely clustered. This is a ship-shape team.

Joshua Allder was known for his 'quiet acts of kindness to the poor', especially in Middle Row, a 'disreputable triangle' of narrow alleyways and overcrowded buildings behind the High Street, where prostitution was rife. Allder's young shopgirls were grateful to escape such a world. The explosion of Croydon's population in the first half of the nineteenth century brought slum conditions to the town centre – but it also ensured the department store's success.

By 1894, Joshua Allder's store occupied nearly an acre in a handsome new building. He helped found West Croydon Baptist Chapel, was elected to the Local Board of Health, and served on the council. He appears frequently on the letters page of the *Croydon Chronicle*, trying to 'awake the town out of its lethargy'. He also persuaded two other North End drapery stores to close at 2 p.m. for a half day on Wednesdays.

In 1908 Allders was sold to Messrs Holdron and Bearman, owners of well-known department stores in Peckham and Leytonstone, and developed into a far slicker business with 50 departments and 500 staff by 1921. The famous North End façade beloved of Croydonians today, with its Portland stone columns and fluttering flags, was built in 1926; a famous, 400-feet arcade was added in 1932 connecting North End to George Street. During the war Allders was badly bombed but never closed, expanding in the 1950s into the neighbouring Scala cinema and installing Croydon's first escalators. In 1958 United Drapery Stores acquired Allders as part of its retail chain, and in 1983 it was sold on to Hanson Trust.

Perhaps Allder's compassion was driven by personal motives, too. Three of his children died at a young age, baby Ada only a year after first opening his store. His wife died at 55. Unlike other department store tycoons he employed just a cook and housemaid for a substantial household. When he died in 1904, Croydon saluted one of its most significant sons with a Cleopatra's needle-type memorial in Queen's Road Cemetery.

From the Allders Facebook page:
'Blimey, Croydon won't be the same.'
'Oh dear, bought Alan's cot from there. Loved the bargain basement.'
'Croydon looks like a ghost town since Allders closed.'

When the Whitgift Centre shopping mall opened next door at the end of the 60s, with Allders effectively as its anchor store, Croydon was confirmed as the biggest shopping centre in the south-east of England. But increasing competition from first Lakeside, then Bluewater and finally Westfield saw shoppers desert Croydon. All the other Allders stores closed in 2005, but the Croydon flagship was saved briefly by Harold Tillman, owner of Jaeger. It closed for good in 2012.

GRANTS 14–22 High Street, Croydon, CR0 • 1877–1985

It is a surreal sight. Soaring over this glorious, mock Queen Anne façade – all stained-glass windows, harlequin brickwork and delicate stone carving – is a vast, barn-like structure concealing a ten-screen cinema. Victorian typography decorates the building's front: *Millinery & Ribbons – Lace & Gloves – Silks & Dresses – Mantles & Linens*. Inside are three chain restaurants, a health club, gym and a nightclub.

Grants' department store – once known as 'the Harrods of Croydon' – is today a 'dedicated leisure destination'. It is also, since 1990, a Grade II-listed building. Croydon's conservationists are still shaking their heads in disbelief that the row of 1890s buildings on the High Street, described by Pevsner as 'the best group of commercial buildings of its date in South London', now serves merely as a facade for this 'bulky monstrosity'. The dominant roofscape is 'overbearing and out of scale,' critics maintain. It detracts from the street's character.

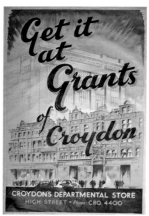

Others see this architectural mash-up as invigorating: Victorian craftsmanship meets modern brutalism. Grants' reincarnation could even be spun as a return to the department store's golden age, when every need was catered for and every dream indulged in a thrilling, fantasy environment. Kennards of Croydon, on nearby North End, was once proud to be known as the store that 'entertained to sell'. Grants Entertainment Centre could simply be seen as a modern continuation of this story.

Brothers Richard and William Grant established their haberdashery on Croydon High Street in 1877. When the road was widened, they started afresh with a lavish, four-storey department store on the opposite site. Architects Metcalfe and Jones threw every embellishment in the book at the new Grant Bros building: gables, oriel windows, turrets, balconies, decorative reliefs in terracotta. Dozens of craftsmen worked on 'London House', as it was known, which was proudly opened in 1895.

Christmas advertising for 1899 suggests the store served Croydon's upper social strata: 'Paste and Steel Buckles, Muff chains, Fancy Hair Combs, Children's Fur

Sets, Opera Capes and Long Cloaks, Dress Lengths for Servants' Presents.' Though Allders would come to be the largest of Croydon's three department stores, Grants would always be the most genteel.

Grants enjoyed another golden era in the inter-war years, when Croydon Airport, with its Art Deco terminal and control tower, opened as Britain's first international airport. French aristocrats flew over just to buy suits from Grants' 'luxurious showrooms'. At the outbreak of war, with the airport soon repurposed as a Battle of Britain station, Grants won the commission to supply all the RAF's uniforms. A local 'Air Raid Spotters' Club' was

hosted within the store. Hundreds of staff left for the war effort. By the war's end, the Grant family was proud to acknowledge two MCs, a DFC and bar, a DSC and three 'mentions' for staff serving in the Forces.

In 1960 the Queen and the Duke of Edinburgh stopped by for tea during their visit to Croydon – but by then, Grants was already in trouble. Croydon Airport had closed the previous year. The department store's clothes were now considered expensive, its offer – top-floor restaurant with thick-pile carpet and linen tablecloths – old-fashioned. Family-owned to the end, Grants closed its doors in 1980.

KENNARDS 11–31 North End, Croydon, CR0 • 1853-1973

When Sir Malcom Campbell's *Blue Bird* broke the world speed record in February 1931, the famous racing car found its way from Daytona Beach in Florida to the ground floor of Kennards in Croydon. Sitting behind the wheel in the publicity shot, hemmed in by ecstatic customers, is the store's managing director Jimmy Driscoll, with his round glasses and signature central parting. Yet again, Driscoll had pulled it off.

'We Entertain to Sell,' went Driscoll's slogan – 'and We Sell to Entertain.' Kennards was the 'Wonder Store of the South'; the house whose publicity stunts made headlines not just in the *Croydon Advertiser*, but internationally. Kennards' reputation was made not by its conservative Victorian founder William Kennard, nor by his two expansionist sons William and Arthur, but by a rank outsider with revolutionary ideas.

Robert 'Jimmy' Driscoll arrived in London from Sydney's department stores in 1911, soon earning a reputation as a genius window dresser both at Barkers and Whiteleys, in time becoming 'the highest paid display specialist in England'. In 1921 the Kennard brothers astutely hired him as general manager for their store. Kennards had been renowned since 1911 for its full-length windows running the length of the building. Driscoll was to be given free rein. Within a month he'd won first prize in the Wolsey All-England Window Display competition for woollen underwear. By the mid-Thirties, Driscoll was 'making the men at Debenham & Freebody, Marshall & Snelgrove and Harvey Nicholls shudder as the latest stories of his exploits circulated'. As the new general manager of Kennards, he would become known as the greatest retail showman of his time.

To promote a 'Jumbo Sale,' Driscoll borrowed two elephants from a Bertram Mills' circus and blocked both ends of the main street, earning himself a court appearance and a write-up in the papers. He introduced 'Clock Days,' when bargains were offered every hour the clock struck. He invented the bi-annual 'Blue Pencil

Week' and, like the Pied Piper, led crowds of shoppers through the store, slashing prices with his blue pencil as he went. Kennards' birthday was celebrated every May with a six-foot-high cake and carnival-like celebrations. Which shopper would spot the 'Mystery Lady', her pockets full of 10 shilling vouchers? Who could prove they were Kennards' 'oldest customer' to win a £25 bedroom suite?

There were Shetland pony rides for children, trit-trotting through the Thirties shopping arcade. A small zoo housed Leo the Lion, Willie the Wolf, Percy the Porcupine and Harry the Hyena, a troop of rhesus monkeys and a sloth. When Joss the baboon escaped from the 'Monkey Village', the vain attempts to capture him on Kennard's rooftop made for great publicity. The rooftop was famous in itself – a 'playground in the sky' with Punch and Judy shows, pitch-and-putt, and a miniature steam railway. In 1932 it hosted 'The most thrilling Wild West Show ever staged in England', with a shoot-out between 'Two-Gun Rix' and

Croydon's new 'playground in the sky', opened 1935.

'Ranger Cliff Norman'.

The year before the war, Mademoiselle Veronica of the Folies Bergère, 'the World's Highest Kicker', visited from Paris to try out the hosiery department's range of stockings, performing 100 high kicks a minute. Soon, however, silk stockings were a distant dream. Kennards was one of the first department stores to offer a service painting stockings onto bare legs, with the promise of 'No More Ladders – All Shades 3d per Leg'. Photographs show male shop assistants (known as 'Kennardians') delicately inscribing seams right up the back of women's legs.

So how did a suburban store manage to hang on to the likes of Jimmy Driscoll, a man who could have had his pick of the West End? When Croydon's first railway station opened in 1839, the local population was 16,000. By 1921 and Driscoll's appointment, it was over 233,000. Kennards was to give the flamboyant Driscoll ten acres of retail space, an eventual 1,200 staff, complete creative control – and shoppers. He

Kennards' annual fancy dress and Christmas parties were a hot ticket. In 1935, some 400 children crammed in to see Cinderella and 'Cardi the Conjuror'.

reigned over 'a town within a store'. He exuded job satisfaction. Even during the dark days of the Blitz, Driscoll's verve and humour didn't flag. In 1943, Kennards' Christmas Grotto was advertising 'the largest Father Christmas in the world: weight, 43 stone, waist, 80 inches'.

Jimmy Driscoll retired in 1950 after 30 years with Kennards. As he told the *Croydon Times*, 'One could not possibly hope to be happier in any walk of life than I have been here.'

Kennards was acquired by the Drapery Trust in 1926, which was absorbed into the Debenhams Empire in 1927, but kept its own brand name and family members until 1973. In the 1980s the site was redeveloped for Croydon's new Drummond Centre, the original building demolished and a new store sited on part of the original footprint. Debenhams announced its closure in 2020.

SHINNERS 71–79 Sutton High Street, Surrey, SM1 • 1899-1992

If you wanted to raise the tone, you booked a table at Shinners. The restaurant's elegant, Art Deco skylight and geometrical patterned carpet were the very latest in Thirties chic. Photographs taken to mark the department store's 1935 re-opening show exquisite interiors down to the grain of the wood, the steel and glass light fittings, the curvy Deco clock on the wall. You can almost imagine Greta Garbo descending the curved wooden stairs from the formal dining room, for this was a department store fit for a Hollywood movie star. And yet this was Sutton, 13 miles from the West End.

Shinners' vast restaurant became Sutton's new social hub, hosting dinners, weddings and fashion shows right into the Sixties. In February 1961, the *Croydon Times* reported on a fashion show of 'gay cottons of startling colour . . . the outfits shown really took the audience away from drab suburbia (and Sutton) into the gay world of sunshine and holidays.'

Whisking customers away from Sutton – and

suburbia – was what Shinners did best. As the town's first department store, opening in the Edwardian era of conspicuous consumption, it strove to tantalise and titillate with the sheer volume of goods and services. No need to head into town: Shinners had it all – from garden spades to corsetry, bicycle pumps to carpet sweepers, manicurists to florists.

Ernest and Fanny Shinner had opened their drapery on Sutton High Street in 1899, aged 24 and 23. Fanny is recorded in the 1911 census as 'assisting in the business': this was a family concern, grown with care, run with pride, eventually ripe for takeover.

But when United Drapery Stores absorbed Shinners in 1927, investment followed. Shareholders were soon being assured that 'building was afoot in Sutton,' while the *Croydon Times* small ads reveal a recruitment drive. Two 'young ladies' were sought as lift attendants – 'must be intelligent and of smart appearance'.

Later, as the war began to bite, Shinners served its loyal community. A clothing alteration workshop opened, along with a second-hand rugs and furniture department. By 1944, the store was offering to repair war-damaged furniture, a representative calling at your

'My mother took us here to get new coats; I was very small, and the store seemed vast and never-ending. We got matching, emerald green coats with black bouclé bobbles and a scarf attached in the same fabric, very elegant. They looked very expensive. As my mother made most of our clothes, these were special.'

Caroline Morris, milliner

home 'without obligation'. During the thrifty Fifties, Shinners had its own workshops with craftsmen for furniture repairs, polishing and building reconstruction.

Happily, there was a return to glamour. One of the benefits of being a United Drapery Store was greater buying power with the major suppliers, and so Shinners stocked 'Charmed Life' nylons by Kayser; it sold exclusive women's fashions also available at D. H. Evans, Swan & Edgar and Woollands up in town. When United Drapery purchased Telstar Colour Television in 1972, Shinners was able to urge its customers to sign up for TV rental at £1.57 a week and watch the Munich Olympics in colour.

Shinners kept its name until 1979, when all United Drapery Stores were gradually renamed Allders to compete with the heft of chains like Debenhams. Many Suttonians continued stubbornly to refer to their department store by its original name – even when the site was taken over by Woolworths in 1994, demolished and rebuilt in clunky red brick. 'Meet you at Shinners', some say to this day, meaning the corner of the High Street and Hill Road. Today the site houses a Waterstone's bookstore – with a café, yes, but no Art Deco fabulousness.

PRATTS

206–224 Streatham High Road, SW16 • 1850–1990

When Grace Hadlow was leaving for hospital to give birth to baby Pauline in 1959, her five-year-old son Graham threw a terrible tantrum. 'Why can't you just go to Pratts?' he wailed. 'You can get anything at Pratts!' After all those visits to their local department store preparing for baby's arrival, he couldn't understand why Pratts wouldn't also sell the finished article.

This is a story about retail and community: how it is fostered, maintained, put to rich use and sustained, against all odds. When Pratts closed in 1990 and was demolished six years later, it felt 'as if the heart had been torn out of the High Road,' wrote one loyal customer. 'Streatham was never the same again.'

Pratts was about people – local people. 'I did my apprenticeship in the hairdressing department 1968–71,' writes one, on a Facebook page for former staff.

'I worked Saturdays and holidays 1973–78,' says another – 'started in electrical, then painting and decorating, soft furnishing and finally menswear.' 'I was a Revlon girl in Pratts in 1980.' 'I was in the Flying Squad, as they called us. When anyone was sick, I'd fill in.' There is a poignancy in scrolling through this 'I Remember Pratts of Streatham' page, knowing that this 500-strong family has now been physically disbanded. For every one of them, working at Pratts was a vivid memory. 'Best years of my life. Mad nights at the social club, brilliant days.'

Many department stores operated paternalistically, 'looking after' their staff with varying degrees of physical, moral and intellectual control. Pratts did it without an eye to benefits accrued. There was a weekly in-house newspaper, *The Chronicle*. There was a sailing club, with a fleet of 36-foot yachts moored at Southampton. There were staff outings to Paris and Amsterdam – and in 1983 'Cathy from Haberdashery' memorably organised an outing to see the Stylistics. Most gloriously, and unusually, there was a staff garden behind the store, a bucolic oasis with lawns and deckchairs, sweet peas and

Relaxing in the staff garden behind the store

delphiniums. When stewed apricots appeared on the dining-room menu, they came from Pratts' own fruit trees.

George Pratt was a young draper's apprentice, originally from Silchester in Hampshire, who bought up his boss's store in Streatham village in around 1850.

The railway arrived in Streatham in 1858, and by 1901 its population had swelled from 7,000 to 71,000. By then, George Pratt and sons were operating from a new, purpose-built emporium called Eldon House, with extra outlets dotted around the High Road as business continued to grow.

In 1919, Pratts was acquired by Bon Marché of Brixton, then by Selfridges Provincial Stores in 1926, and finally the John Lewis Partnership in 1940. Staff cameraderie was strengthened during the Second World War when Pratts became a venue for community fund-raising events for the war effort, providing parcels for serving Partners, dinners for ARP teams and concerts for merchant seamen. Thus Pratts, which escaped the Blitz, cemented its status as a beacon of the local community, guaranteeing unshakable loyalty and affection long after the War.

Perhaps, ultimately, it didn't matter who owned Pratts. It was Streatham that made the store special.

Pratts was closed by the John Lewis Partnernship, after years of rumour and speculation, on Saturday, 28 July 1990. One month later, a four-storey John Lewis opened

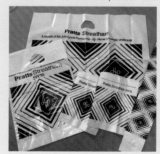

in Kingston-upon-Thames. The Pratts building was demolished in 1996, the site redeveloped to house Lidl and Argos in a redbrick nonentity. In the words of former shopgirl Christine, 'hideous'.

Career Women

Evelyn Whiteside

'One of the cleverest buyers in the trade,' Scotswoman Evelyn Whiteside started her career in fashion as a house model at Debenham & Freebody. She ended up as the first female director of Fortnums – and the only female director of a West End store.

'I don't care if she's young and inexperienced,' blustered Sir Woodman Burbidge in 1935, having taken her on as a Harrods fashion buyer aged 23. 'What we need is someone with taste, and I know she's got that.' From then on she was known simply as 'Whiteside', working for a tyrant in the sportswear department, learning the hard way the Golden Rule: 'Never overspend your season's allocation.' Having increased Harrods' turnover by £2,000 a year, she moved on to build up the women's department at Simpson Piccadilly.

Her career peaked at Fortnum & Mason where she revolutionised the rather staid, luxury grocery store by introducing high fashion from 1947. By the late 1950s Whiteside had become a powerful celebrity in her own right, photographed in a £2,400 mink coat for the *Tatler* and sharing her Christmas wish list (a continuous supply of Asti Spumante and a 'monster box' of *Marrons Glacés*).

Evelyn Whiteside – who had no children, but many godchildren – was widowed in her late forties. She claimed to 'despise' aggressive feminism, 'especially in wives'. On the whole, she said, in a 1960 interview, 'Men should be the bosses.' Her secret weapon in the boardroom was 'good grooming' – 'an essential part of a businesswoman's equipment'.

Irene Stephens

In the 1960s the John Lewis Partnership offered great opportunities to career-minded women. Irene Mary Stephens had the necessary tenacity, dependability and good humour. Her long

and illustrious career there started in middle age as 'Miss Crane' in the furniture department at Peter Jones.

Within two years, she was promoted to General Manager, Merchandise, then moved to buying 'Regulation School Dress'. Marrying rather late, she arrived at Pratts in Streatham as Mrs Stephens, General Manager (always surnames, never first names). Former staff still remember the huge party she organised for the store's centenary at the nightclub above Streatham Ice Rink.

In her fifties, Irene continued to climb the ladder: Director of Buying, Fashion Accessories; Chief Registrar (director level); member of the Central Council, before retiring in 1983. She is talked about still.

BON MARCHÉ

442–444 Brixton Road, SW9; 244–250 Ferndale Road · 1877–1975

Britain's first purpose-built department store was the result of an almost inconceivable double win at the races. In 1876, a four-year-old colt called Roseberry scooped both the Cesarewitch and the Cambridgeshire stakes at Newmarket. She belonged to a printer from Tooting – Mr James Smith, owner of the *Sportsman* newspaper – who decided to invest his £80,000 winnings in a bold foray into commerce. He would

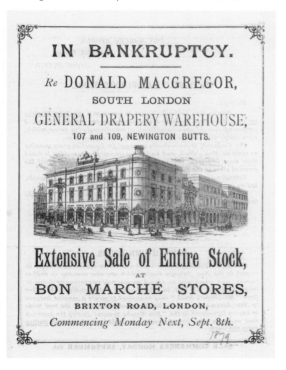

build a grand department store on his home turf.

James 'Roseberry' Smith (as he became known) had a good eye for horseflesh, but knew nothing about retail. Pumped up with his new wealth and celebrity, he set about engaging Lambeth architects Parsons & Rawlings to re-create, at breakneck speed, the greatest department store of them all. Smith decided he would even borrow the name.

Le Bon Marché of rue de Sèvres, Paris, was famous the world over. Founded in 1838, and spectacularly revamped by Aristide Boucicaut in 1852, it was one of the first modern department stores. By 1877 – when Mr Smith's upstart Brixton store opened for business – this great Parisian phenomenon was employing some 1,800 employees, running over 74 departments, and making 72 million francs a year. The subject of Zola's novel *Au Bonheur des Dames* ('The Ladies Paradise'), it

was 'an ever-humming machine', exerting 'an unsettling neurosis' on its helpless female shoppers.

To steal this illustrious name for an entrepreneurial gamble in Brixton smacked, frankly, of hubris. Yet you couldn't fault Smith for his ambition, or his efforts to imitate the original, from the Baroque detailing to the internal sweeping staircases and wrought-iron balconies, to the paternalistic owner culture.

Aristide and Marguerite Boucicault had, like Smith, come from humble origins. They pioneered social benefits such as company-owned housing, free evening training courses and a pension fund. Similarly in Brixton, impressive staff living quarters were created in Toplin House on Ferndale Road, next to the Astoria Cinema (which is now the Brixton Academy music venue), connected to the store by single-sex underground tunnels 70 metres in length (and used as bomb shelters during the Second World War).

Parisian trading methods were also copied on the shop floor: fixed low prices, no haggling and plenty of choice. Local shops couldn't compete. One Brixton tradesman was said to have been so afraid he would lose his customers to the Bon Marché that he committed suicide.

With the chutzpah of a gambler, 'Roseberry' Smith was determined to secure the best of everything. He'd heard of a newfangled pneumatic tube system that circulated money and receipts around the building: the Lamson. He had to have it. Brixton's Bon Marché joined Robinson & Cleaver of Regent Street and Roberts of

Stratford as its first adopters. And because Bon Marché of Paris had a famously efficient mail order service, Smith craved one too. Partnering with a Mr Saunders, he created an almost Amazon-like service, which guaranteed to open every order and despatch the goods within one hour.

But did Victorian Brixton – never prosperous or fashionable – need a department store with Parisian aspirations? It appears that Smith had over-estimated local demand. Within 15 years he was declared bankrupt, with debts of £71,000.

Going, going: the last hurrah for Bon Marché staff, 1975.

The store was saved from closure in 1892 by five experienced retailers who made it a public company. Slowly but steadily, with plush fitted carpets, many more fashion departments, a handsome arcade and tearooms, they built up its reputation – then started buying up the local competition. Pratts of Streatham was acquired in 1919, neighbouring rival Quin & Axtens the following year. Selfridge Provincial Stores bought all three in 1926, to be absorbed by the John Lewis Partnership in 1940.

Despite suffering terrible bomb damage in 1941, Bon Marché revived and remained popular with the local community. But in 1975 wan-faced staff were told that their store 'didn't fit well into the Partnership's vision for the future'. A humdinger of a leaving party was held on Monday, 2 June; by Saturday evening the store had closed.

The building and its signage are still with us, along with Toplin House and its landmark tower. After a chequered  modern history, including a spate of failed indoor market projects, the space was split up into retail concession units, attracting brands such as TopShop and sparking the regeneration of Brixton town centre. Today it is anchored by TK Maxx and the Bon Marché Business Centre. Meanwhile, Toplin House was rescued from squatters in 2015 and imaginatively stripped back to its shell by architects Squire & Partners. It is now leased to a variety of creative and retail businesses and known as 'The Department Store'.

QUIN & AXTENS
422–440 Brixton Road, SW9 • 1880–1941

Quin & Axtens was Bon Marché's neighbour and bitter rival.

If Bon Marché dropped its silk prices, Quin & Axtens was compelled to push lower. When Bon Marché staged a Christmas parade, the rival Santa Claus scaled *his* shop front and climbed in by a window. Quin & Axtens' winter sales opened a week earlier than Bon Marché's; it was the store that sold 'the best value gramophones in London'. This ongoing rivalry gave Brixton Road a feverish buzz, ablaze with banners and hoardings trying to catch the eye.

To South London shoppers, 'Quin & Axtens' Bazaar' was the slightly less sumptuous and keener-priced destination, despite a grand, wrought-iron corner entrance topped by a dome. At the time of the store's

takeover by Bon Marché in 1920, large banners can be seen advertising 'Display of Stylish Costumes for 21/-', 'Smart Shirts for 2/11' and 'Boots for 10/-'. Co-founder William Axtens and his wife Mabel (a court dressmaker, and daughter of the Green's Chocolate Blancmange family) threw up their hands and graciously accepted defeat. In any case, Mr Axtens remained very much in charge.

Little is known of his original business partner Cornelius Quin, who ran a drapery shop at 430 Brixton Road from 1873 onwards. When William Axtens bought into partnership with Quin in 1887 he was already 60 years old, and retired shortly afterwards. 'Quin & Axtens' had a pleasing ring to it. The name stuck.

In 1926, Selfridge Provincial Stores Group acquired the business, along with neighbouring Bon Marché and Pratts of Streatham. Quin & Axtens got an immediate rebuild in the Selfridges classical style, with huge, plate glass 'island windows' created by multiple entry points. These it put to immediate effect: a demonstration in 'expert glovemaking' occupied a prime spot in

Brixton Road, S.W. Corner of Stockwell Road.

November 1928, where two 'highly skilled workers' from famous glovemakers Fownes of Worcester showed crowds 'exactly how it was done'.

The new-look store had a fatally short life. One year after joining the John Lewis Partnership, it was completely gutted by an enemy bomb during the Blitz. Wednesday, 16 April 1941 turned out to be Quin & Axtens' last day of trading. 'Quin & Axtens destroyed by enemy action' ran a notice in the *Norwood News*, as Brixton struggled to carry on after that catastrophic night. 'BON MARCHÉ Brixton carry on for them. Quin & Axtens' customers will find very many of the staff and almost all the stocks that they knew there at BON

MARCHÉ next door. The Communal Feeding Centre, doubled in size, opens in BON MARCHÉ shortly.'

In truth, Bon Marché had been propping up its former rival Quin & Axtens for many decades now. The *coup de grâce* was swift and, just possibly, timely.

ARDING & HOBBS

315 Lavender Hill, SW11 • 1884–2020

Arding & Hobbs was – and still is – 'part of Clapham Junction's DNA'. With its prime spot at the junction of Lavender Hill and St John's Road, and the landmark clock tower familiar to millions of commuters, it is a 'community hub', locals declare; 'the heart of Battersea.' Its closure in 2020, as part of the collapse of Debenhams, was greeted with disbelief and dismay.

Residents were more deeply shaken over a century ago, when the store burned to the ground in one of London's most sensational shop fires. The blaze broke out on the ground floor blouse department at 4.30 p.m., 20 December 1909, rampaging through the building with frightening speed thanks to the reams of Christmas decorations. Within ten minutes the store was 'a roaring furnace', the flames so fierce they roasted the turkeys in the butcher's shop opposite. Male and female shop assistants, trapped and screaming in their quarters on the top floor, tried to escape by jumping from windows. Eight died. Press photographs the following morning show crowds gathered in shock before the ravaged silhouette: they couldn't imagine Clapham Junction without Arding & Hobbs. They couldn't imagine life without Arding & Hobbs.

But this was the thrusting Edwardian era, and the calamity spawned opportunity. 'The Great Fire at Clapham Junction. £250,000 Damage' – ran an advertisement in the *Westminster Gazette* on New Year's Eve. 'The whole of Messrs. Arding and Hobbs books, documents, cash, banknotes and cheques preserved intact in SIX JOHN TANN'S Anchor Reliance Safes and Strong Room. THE ONLY SAFES IN USE. Illustrated Catalogue Post-Free, JOHN TANN, Newgate Street EC.'

Earlier that same year the opening of Selfridges had shaken up department stores throughout the capital.

> 'I remember the old lifts with uniformed "lift boys" in them. Before they put escalators in.' – *Denise Cook*

GREAT FIRE AT ARDING AND HOBBS DEC 20 1909

Bold and elegant transformations were springing off architect's pages. Why not Arding & Hobbs?

William Arding and James Hobb had started their drapery business in 1876, first with one store in Wandsworth, then another in Battersea. Lavender Hill was their third site, opened in 1884 when Clapham Junction was still a backwater. Thanks to the railway, this was soon to change. By the turn of the century, the three stores had combined on this one, lucrative spot.

James Hobbs retired in 1905 – and so, after the fire, Henry Arding had *carte blanche* to create a department

store for the twentieth century. Not for him a local architect. The new Arding & Hobbs needed to stop the middle-class Battersea housewife travelling over the river to the West End. He engaged James Gibson, the talent behind the Baroque-revival rebuild of Debenham & Freebody in 1907.

The new department store opened one year later in the Edwardian Baroque style: four storeys in red brick and Bath stone with elaborate carvings, two tiers of magnificent show windows. There was a sweeping main staircase (lost in the 1960s refurb). Ferrier's Blue

'Fairy caves' and a giant lake at the lavish Christmas Grotto, 1930s.

Viennese Band played daily in the upstairs restaurant, which was lit by a beautiful stained-glass dome. It's

In 1981 Arding & Hobbs was 'blown up' in the opening titles of *Nighthawks*, a Sylvester Stallone action movie set in New York. Three years later it served as a surreal refuge for the lone survivor of an apocalypse in the Human League's video for their hit single 'Life on Your Own'. A decade later the store was memorably visited by Rowan Atkinson in *Do-it-Yourself Mr Bean* (1994), parking his lime green Mini on the pavement outside and jumping the queue for the sales.

there to this day. Rooms on upper floors were set aside for banquets and balls; there was even a Masonic Temple. Rising proudly above it all, at the street's corner, was a gilded, stone-clad octagonal tower, destined to become one of Battersea's most iconic architectural monuments.

In October 1939 Arding & Hobbs amalgamated with the John Anstiss Group of eight department stores from Worthing to Cirencester; perhaps not the best time to begin a business expansion venture. Soon, staff

Acquired in 2018 by commercial property specialists W.RE, Arding & Hobbs is undergoing a 'sensitive' transformation. The building is being renovated 'back to its 1920s glory', with original features exposed and the travesties of 1960s and '70s refurbs stripped out, to create new retail, leisure and office space. A modernist new rooftop extension will also be added, changing the skyline. The project, which has already garnered plaudits, is something of a test case in the repurposing of old department stores.

were leaving in droves for the war effort. Post-war, the United Drapery Stores swallowed the group in 1948. By the 1980s, Arding & Hobbs' lack of outside parking had begun to deter shoppers, and another retail giant, Allders, intervened – before going bust in 2005, when Arding & Hobbs passed to Debenhams PLC.

Were residents aware of their store's more recent chequered history? Probably not. As long as the grand edifice was still standing; as long as you could reliably pop in for a pair of evening shoes, a new sofa, a cup of tea or a Pyrex casserole dish, all was right in SW11. When Debenhams' collapse sealed its fate, *Guardian* columnist Polly Toynbee eulogised the store as 'the pride of Battersea, the delight for decades of my life'.

The Department Store as Theatre

No one had a better instinct for showmanship and newspaper headlines than Harry Gordon Selfridge. In July 1909, four months after Selfridges had opened on Oxford Street, Louis Blériot's monoplane went on display in the store – the very morning after he'd made history by crossing the Channel. It was a sensational coup. A hundred and fifty thousand people came to see the plane over four days, with queues around the block. On the final day Selfridges stayed open until midnight.

The 1920s and 30s was an era obsessed with land and water speed records, and pioneering long-distance flying. Selfridge repeated his coup by displaying other machines of derring-do: Sir Henry Segrave's *Golden Arrow* racing car, Amy Johnson's biplane, *Gipsy Moth*, and Malcolm Campbell's *Blue Bird* racing car. Where Selfridge led, others followed. Competition between London's department stores soon rose to a fevered pitch.

Kennards of Croydon built up a reputation during the 30s for its quirky publicity stunts, from cheetahs

Max and Moritz, Kennards of Croydon's chimpanzeees, could walk a tightrope, stunt cycle and roller-skate (mid-1930s).

in the restaurant to snake charmers on the roof. Its greatest rival was Bentalls of Kingston, ten miles to the west (still trading today as part of the Fenwick Group). Driven by the competitive personalities of Kennards' MD Jimmy Driscoll and Bentalls' publicity director Eric Fleming, the two stores waged a running battle for the most headline grabbing 'tie-in,' as publicity stunts were known, to generate newspaper copy. Campbell's *Blue Bird* came to Bentalls too (as well as

Malcolm Campbell's record-breaking *Blue Bird* **at Gamages, 1932.**

Kennards): the Campbell family lived locally.

But it was Fleming who took advantage of Bentalls' vast, glass roofed escalator atrium to stage perhaps the most spectacular stunt of all. Twice daily for a fortnight, a diminutive young Swedish woman performed an astonishing diving feat.

Anita Kittner would climb a wall-mounted ladder until her head almost touched the glass roof. At this point the suspenseful music would stop, abruptly. Bentalls customers, packing the ground floor and upper floor balconies, held their breaths. Miss Kittner threw down her shoes, crawled out on all fours to the end of the diving board and slowly rose to a handstand. Finally, after holding the pose for some seconds, she let out a blood-curdling scream and dived – aiming at a pool just ten foot wide and five foot deep. Her safe emergence from the water was greeted with gasps of relief and resounding applause.

Kittner's first Bentalls engagement in 1937 proved so popular she was invited back in 1939.

Anita Kittner, Swedish stunt diver, 1930s.

ARMY & NAVY 101 Victoria Street, SW1 • 1871–2022

'The British Parliament is one institution, the Stores are another,' wrote department store connoisseur 'Olivia' in 1906. 'Ask "where should I buy – anything?" and you know the answer before it is spoken: "The Stores".' No other reference was needed. No other London department store seems to have generated such loyalty, generation after generation. 'It was the pre-Amazon Amazon,' remembers one wistful shopper, who would drive up from Sussex in the 1980s to do

his Christmas shopping, park behind the Stores, lunch in the restaurant, and leave with a car boot stuffed full of gift-wrapped presents.

This store was the mother ship of a chain that stretched around the British Empire. In colonial India there were six Army & Navy Co-operative Stores Ltd, the last closing in Bombay in 1952. 'Get your make of shoe registered, and you may go to China and still be served with shoes from the Stores,' writes Olivia. 'Indeed, go anywhere in the world and the benefits of the Stores will follow you.' In Britain there were over 30 branches – mostly in places with military connections such as Aldershot, Camberley, Chatham and Plymouth.

It began in London in 1871 with a few cases of wine. A group of army officers clubbed together to buy port and sherry at wholesale prices, and the business swiftly took off, opening on Victoria Street the following year. The officers branched out into golf clubs, sporting guns, leather goods and cigars – anything a man of officer class might like to get his hands on. Shareholders (military men and their families) were entitled to deal at the store, share in profits and enjoy free delivery. Members, who paid half a crown for an

The modern building opened in 1977.

annual subscription, had no such privileges.

By the turn of the century, 'The Stores' could look after its 50,000 members from cradle to grave. They would find you a house or a flat, provide you with laundry services and coals for the fire, even find someone to wind up your grandfather clock while you were away. From the 1,000-page catalogue you could order anything from dinner gongs, to laxatives, to ear trumpets, trusses and hair-restorer. 'Tea may be bought next door to tea gowns,' observed Olivia, 'bacon next to summer muslins, organdies next to account books.'

The Victorian building was unusual, having no display windows until 1922. Inside and out it had the air of a club. It was a matter of pride that staff recognized members and addressed them by name, even if they had been overseas in the colonies for years. There was even, famously, a porter at the front entrance to look after members' dogs. 'It is an institution of justice and contentment,' wrote Olivia. But was it really?

When, on the morning of 3 December 1919, customers found no dog minder at the entrance, it was a sign that all was not well within. In the biggest retail strike in history, A&N staff bought the institution to its knees over their onerous working conditions and poor pay.

The resulting agreement revolutionised working conditions for retail staff across the industry.

In 1973, the Army & Navy was absorbed into House of Fraser and the membership scheme ended. The nineteenth-century department store in Victoria Street was knocked down and rebuilt with a modern, boxy façade of bronze tinted glass, opening in 1977. It carried the A&N name until 2005, when the chain was renamed 'House of Fraser'. The store closed for good in January 2022, to be demolished and redeveloped as shops and offices.

JUNIOR ARMY & NAVY
15 Regent Street, W1 · 1880–1920

Major Clench was an Army & Navy member who got embroiled in a dispute over share-holding rights and left to set up on his own in Regent Street, successfully defending a lawsuit over his use of the name. The two rival businesses co-existed for forty years, greatly confusing the general public, but never their loyal customers. As with a club, you belonged to either one or the other.

York House – or Club Chambers, as it was also known – was a very grand building, with

two passenger elevators, allegedly the first in the country. Connoisseurs deemed it more go-ahead: 'The Junior Army & Navy is no mean rival of the older establishment,' noted a shopping guide for 1890: 'It is on the whole the most enterprising of the Stores.'

The rules for selling and for membership were a little more lax: travellers from America or the Colonies could gain access simply by purchasing a ticket for 2s.19d, upon introduction from a member. Indeed, perhaps the whole modus operandi was more lax: in 1882 the Junior Army & Navy was found guilty of infringing the copyright of Maple & Co. by reproducing their furniture illustrations in its catalogue.

By 1900, the company had 600 employees and five branches around London. In 1909, as with other co-operatives, the rules were changed so that the general public could shop here. But it remained closely affiliated to the armed forces, calling itself 'America's Blighty Store' during the Great War, the best place for soldiers to get their kit.

After the war the Regent Street store was gripped by strike fever – but its workers didn't bargain on their wage demands triggering its demise. Having already amalgamated with the Civil Service Co-operative Stores in 1919, Junior Army and Navy closed York House in 1920.

Admiralty storeship *Borodino*, contracted to the Junior Army & Navy during the First World War.

GORRINGES
75 Buckingham Palace Road, SW1 • 1858-1968

During the summer sales of 1885, an upper housemaid from Buckingham Palace entered Gorringes department store. There was nothing unusual in this; Gorringes was known as the Palace's village shop, a well-known haunt of staff on imperative, quick errands for haberdashery or sewing thread. Margaret Plater was a well-dressed woman of 49; beyond suspicion you might think.

NEW PREMISES
FREDERICK GORRINGES L.
BUCKINGHAM PALACE R.º SW.

But the store detective was watching her. Plater emerged insouciantly from the gentleman's bag department with a black bag over her arm, bearing a 'Sale' ticket. She walked about the bazaar department for five minutes before taking up a red plush bag from the counter and secreting it inside the black bag. From here, she went upstairs to the lace room. The detective followed at a discreet distance.

Margaret Plater was accosted by a Gorringes manager, and claimed complete innocence. She must, she said, have lost her receipts. But the woman was searched, and found also to have a sponge in her pocket, still with its sale ticket. Buckingham Palace's upper housemaid was brought before Westminster Police Court, where the Queen's Head Housekeeper stood bail for £40, describing Plater as being of 'irreproachable character.' She was found guilty at trial, and sentenced to two months in prison.

On balance, the association with the Palace brought

Women, Shops and Shoplifting

Shoplifting, or 'kleptomania', was rife in department stores. The offenders were ostensibly well-to-do women who succumbed to shop-window temptation – all those luxuries displayed behind glass, expressly calculated to arouse desire . . . London had, since the 1880s, been transformed into a space where it was acceptable for middle-class women to engage in conspicuous consumption. But could they control their impulses?

In 1888 *The Draper's Record* questioned the wisdom of the so-called 'Parisian system': the 'walk-around store', as opposed to old-fashioned counter service. Was the open display of luxury goods a 'moral threat' to female customers? Shoplifting arrests soared just before Christmas, and during the summer and winter sales, when shops were 'uncomfortably thronged'.

Ten years later, the *Millinery Record* recommended hiring 'private enquiry staff' or dedicated store detectives to keep an eye on women customers, as it was impossible for assistants or shop walkers 'to efficiently attend to the requirements of impatient customers and at the same time keep anything like a sharp eye on the knavish tricks and wiles of the expert shoplifter'.

A Gorringes sales assistant demonstrates the new vacuum cleaner technology, 1910. Department stores were drivers of labour-saving devices, helping wealthier customers hang on to – or dispense with – their servants.

Gorringes more prestige than it did problems. Its proximity (the only department store to be situated in Buckingham Palace Road) fostered a culture of

'My great, great aunt Carrie Norris worked at Gorringes from 1875 until the 1930s, when she was in her seventies. She was an assistant in the lace department, and lived in the rooms for single staff on the top floor all that time. I wonder whether she acted as some sort of "house mother" to the single young staff, what with being there so long?' – *Pete, Rootschat*

Section of Ladies' Hairdressing Dept. at Gorringes

absolute servility among Frederick Gorringe's staff, renowned for their deferential service. His store assistants were forbidden to sit down behind the counter (even after the Seats for Shop Assistants Act of 1899 ensured a chair behind every counter). They were forbidden to speak to customers, unless spoken to first. There was a strict dress code, and unmarried staff lived in – in tiny rooms at the top of the store.

More cheeringly, the daily march past by the Guards' band in their bearskins lifted staff spirits right into the 1960s. Staff requests for special tunes were discreetly accepted, especially on birthdays.

In 1908 an immense, red-brick, Edwardian building replaced Gorringe's piecemeal Victorian incarnation, advertised as 'Two minutes from Victoria Station'. Dedicated trains were laid on from Brighton, but

Gorringe's bread and butter remained its smart Belgravia clients, many with country houses to run. Cecil Mills, who joined the store in 1926, remembered serving ladies placing large orders for their servants: 300 pairs of socks and stockings; dozens of cardigans for gardeners and stablemen, all in the same staff livery.

Post-war, Gorringes began to seem less smart, and its customers more provincial, timid, loyal and elderly. In 1965 – the year of *Help!* by the Beatles – the *Tatler* reported on the store's new boutique collection. The illustration shows a double pleated skirt with collarless jacket tied with patent bow belt, cost 52 guineas. It was the sort of outfit a mother might choose for her daughter.

A bleak and boxy 1960 rebuild looked more like a prison than a department store. After 110 years of good old-fashioned service, Gorringes finally disappeared at the end of 1968. In the High Court, the store was claimed to owe £77,000 in rent.

WOOLLANDS 95–107 Knightsbridge, SW1 • 1869 –1967

In the 1950s, Knightsbridge's two department stores were dowdy, dependable and predictable – a place for elderly aunts to meet amid the potted palms. Harvey Nichols was known as 'the old ladies' store', while its next-door neighbour, Woollands, was 'the forgotten one.' Which of these once great Edwardian stores would survive?

The Woolland Brothers (Samuel and William) had already pulled off one re-invention. Their original

'servants bazaar' of the Victorian era had by 1902 – with judicious window displays and an eye to women's fashion – become *the* place for peeresses to buy their Coronation robes. Business was now conducted from a grand new building, clad in Baroque Portland stone, far more elaborate in style than that of rival Harvey Nichols. The Duchess of Portland shopped here, as did Edward VII's mistress Alice Keppel.

For Edwardian shopping correspondent 'Olivia', picking her fastidious way through the capital in 1906, Woollands takes the palm: 'My favourite shop in London. Someone is at the head of affairs who has a most delicious sense of colour. The very carpets on the floors at Woollands give this away. When this deliciousness runs into ribbons and chiffon . . .'

Yet, by 1954, Woollands was a sea of beige conformity. Enter Martin Moss, a 31-year-old retail executive appointed general manager. Moss started a revolution that turned the store into a showcase for young talent and set the trend for the retail era of swinging London. America's influential *Women's Wear Daily* called him 'London's one-man wave of fashion'.

Out went the beige; in came the psychedelic colours

of Pucci, Balenciaga and Givenchy. Moss employed a 22-year-old, Vanessa Denza (left), to launch the 21 Shop, a ground-floor boutique aimed at style-conscious teenagers. Denza brought in new, young designers from the Royal College of Arts to create affordable fashion: Sally Tuffin and Marion Foale, Gerald McCann, Ossie Clark.

The opening evening show in 1961, in a pine-clad

department designed by the young Terence Conran, was a triumph (and, laughed Denza, 'a shoplifter's paradise'). Crowds queued round the block; inside, Vidal Sassoon-coiffed models sashayed down the runway to the sounds of the Temperance Seven.

Martin Moss revolutionised the staid furniture floor, bringing in the best of Scandinavian and Finnish design, plus Terence Conran furniture, to create semi-room sets. Down in the basement, kitchenware was transformed into objects of desire by the use of imaginative shop fitting and a huge cast-iron cooking range, evoking Elizabeth David's *A Book of Mediterranean Food* (1950). Suddenly, baskets, casseroles, knives, pots and pans became fashion items.

Moss ensured a vibrant, new lease of life for Woollands, placing it at the heart of modern London. But could two big department stores survive, side by side?

Debenham & Freebody had acquired Harvey Nichols in 1920 and Woollands in 1949, running the stores as separate entities. By the mid-1960s, it was unrealistic to keep both. Despite its success, Woollands was the chosen casualty; the site was extremely valuable. The store closed in 1967 and was demolished in 1969 to make way for

the Sheraton Park Tower Hotel rotunda (dismissed by architecture critics as a 'scent bottle'). Martin Moss jumped ship to become MD of Simpson Piccadilly, while most of his staff went next door to Harvey Nichols.

Urban Landmarks by Design

London's earliest department stores weren't designed: they were knocked together. The result was a rabbit warren of twisting corridors and uneven ceilings easy to get lost in (Gamages of Holborn remained that way until it closed in the 1970s). But as soon they began to be constructed from the ground up, each had to be architecturally state-of-the-art: the most modern and striking edifice around; instantly monumental; demanding that the shopper take all their custom there. Over the ensuing twentieth century, department stores have contributed some of the most landmark architecture to the streets of the capital.

MESSRS. DEBENHAM & FREEBODY'S NEW PREMISES.
Photographed from a Model exhibited at the Franco-British Exhibition.
BUILDERS: MESSRS. GEORGE TROLLOPE & SONS and COLLS & SONS, LTD.
ARCHITECTS: MESSRS. WILLIAM WALLACE & J. S. GIBSON.

above: **Baroque Revival**
Debenham & Freebody, 1907. A colonnaded palace with elaborate turret, clad entirely in Doulton's carrara ware tiles. 'Quite one of the sights of the West End', thought the *American Register*. Eclipsed, two years later, by Selfridges.

left: **Beaux-Arts**
Selfridges, 1909. Ionic columns hiding an early steel frame, designed by Daniel Burnham – the American architect behind Chicago's Marshall Fields. The *Daily Express* likened it to the opening of 'a national exhibition or museum or gallery of art'.

Edwardian Wrenaissance
Waring & Gillow, 1906. The first West End store to occupy a whole block. 'The new Warings is an ornament to Oxford Street, with its towering height and its façade in red brick and Portland Stone, modelled upon the Palace at Hampton Court' – *Daily Telegraph*, 1906.

Early Art Deco
Drages, Oxford Street, 1929. Epitomises the brash and exuberant spirit of interwar commercial flash, with its sculptural decoration in pink on grey. 'Of notable excellence', thought the *Architect and Building News* in 1930, with elements of 'fantasie', 'surprise' and 'intriguing Gallic gaiety'. (Demolished 2014.)

Moderne
Simpson Piccadilly, 1936. A modernist masterpiece in Portland stone and glass by Joseph Emberton. 'An excellent, progressive piece of store design . . . here is an architect who handles the new idiom with conviction and personality' – Nikolaus Pevsner, *The Buildings of England*.

Brutalist

Peter Robinson, Strand, 1958. The first post-war building in England to make large-scale use of bronze cladding; critic Ian Nairn thought it 'The only new shop in London to match up to Peter Jones' (Sloane Square, 1936). Its architect, Denys Lasdun, went on to design the National Theatre. (Demolished 1996.)

Generic plate-glass box

House of Fraser Westfield, 2008. Corporate, anonymous architecture for a mall containing three other department stores and 300 retail outlets 'all under one roof'. 'Post pandemic, shopping malls need to make a sensual connection with the customer in order to survive,' says retail consultant Mary Portas.

Last throw of the dice

Debenhams Oxford Street, 2013. A £25 million store revamp, with glass corners and roof.

BARKERS 63 Kensington High Street, W8 · 1870-2006

The 'Barkerisation' of Kensington High Street was a term coined by irate residents of Kensington Square who, by the 1920s, had had enough of the constant flow of delivery vans up and down Young Street, the endless cranes, demolition, rebuilding, road closure – even the entire building over of a road (Ball Street), as John Barker & Co.'s W8 kingdom grew ever larger.

Today, seeing just the immense Art Deco building at the end of Kensington Church Street, you might conclude that this was the extent of it. But in 1926,

when yet another Barkers building went up, this time on the north side of Kensington High Street, it was felt that the department store empire had colonised too much of the neighbourhood, above and below ground. A warren of subways now linked the new 'Ladymere' store with that of the mother ship opposite. Retail neighbours Derry & Toms and Pontings also belonged to John Barker & Co. More plans were flying off the paper for extensive rebuilding, pushing the store facades back by 30 feet, creating pavements built for window gazers.

Customers – some 50,000 a day – were willingly 'Barkerised'. Each store had its own distinct identity,

creating a range of appeal as broad as anything on Oxford Street. Barkers signalled 'high class', Derry & Toms represented 'good middle class', while Pontings traded as 'The House for Value'. Sir John Barker made the shopping Mecca of High Street Kensington. How did he do it?

A man in the entrepreneurial mould of William Whiteley and Arthur Gamage, Barker is one of the great personalities of the London department store story. He became a public figure: Sir John Barker, a Liberal MP

Barkers' elegant depository.

with a baronetcy and wax-tipped moustache, lionised by the Society magazine *Vanity Fair*, the owner of a 300-acre Hertfordshire estate and breeder of polo ponies and Syrian sheep. It was quite a journey for a brewer's son from Kent.

Barker came to London in the 1850s, cut his teeth at Whiteley's, then struck out on his own, leasing the first of his Kensington properties in 1870. So began

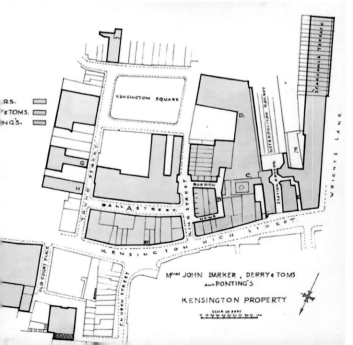

Mrs JOHN BARKER, DERRY & TOMS
AND PONTING'S

KENSINGTON PROPERTY

an insatiable colonisation as his store swelled in size. Kensington High Street had already attracted other drapers: Joseph Toms and his brother-in-law Charles Derry went into partnership in 1862, and in 1873 the four Ponting Brothers – Thomas, William, Sydney and John – set up shop. All three businesses expanded rapidly, annexing shop after shop, diversifying their merchandise.

By the coronation of King Edward VII in 1902, John Barker & Co was operating one of the largest emporia in London. One-and-a-half thousand staff serviced 64 departments; delivery vans despatched 2,000 parcels daily. Like William Whiteley and Arthur Gamage, Barker liked to cut out the middleman and source direct from manufacturers. He took pride that his store was 'devoted to the supply of all classes of goods at the lowest possible prices'.

Business faltered in 1912 when a fire destroyed half the premises, ending in an inquest over the tragic death of five waitresses who'd jumped from their top-floor rooms. Sir John died in 1914, spared the worry of the wartime slump. Unprofitable departments were closed, wages reduced and the delivery service cut back after the sale of 100 horses to the War Office.

The company's fortunes revived with two more visionary personalities, men who understood that shopping had changed fundamentally since the Great War. As Chairman Sir Sydney Skinner saw it, shopping

was now 'a recreation as much as a duty'. Barkers had already acquired Pontings in 1907; Derry & Toms followed in 1920. Skinner's mission was to create an entity that could take on Oxford Street. 'We want higher buildings,' he declared, 'more imposing buildings, buildings that are spacious with uninterrupted vistas, pleasing to the senses . . .'

His masterstroke was to push for the widening of Kensington High Street, a choked bottleneck where you window-gazed at your peril. This required, perforce, a total rebuild of Derry & Toms (completed 1933), and of Barker's (interrupted by the war, finally completed in 1958).

Skinner's right-hand man was MD Trevor Bowen, originally a confectioner from Monmouth. 'The customer is not an *interruption* of our work,' Bowen liked to say; 'he is the *purpose* of it.' Here was the force behind the Derry & Toms roof garden, opened in 1938; a fantasy environment inspired by Bowen's tour of the great department stores of America.

The new Barkers store began to rise in 1936, designed by in-house architect Bernard George, who was also responsible for Derry & Toms. The two buildings, though both Art Deco in style, are strikingly different neighbours. Barkers embodies the bold changes in British taste of the early 1930s, especially in the architecture of shopping. Bernard George was alert to the European Expressionist styles made popular by the Paris Exhibition of 1924: the distortion of form for emotional effect. He experimented with contemporary Scandinavian design, using gilt metalwork on the window frames. Quaint department store goods decorate the strips between windows: cricket pads, washing pails.

The great rebuild was two-thirds done before war intervened, the rest finished 1955–8. In 1957, an elderly Bowen sold the Barkers Group to the Scottish draper

entrepreneur, Hugh Fraser – someone who would 'keep faith with the Barker tradition'. From the 60s, Barkers was credited with pioneering the celebrity book signing, with authors from Peter Ustinov (left) to Diana Dors inscribing their new volume.

In the House of Fraser rationalisation that followed, Pontings closed first in 1970, followed by Derry & Toms in 1973 (still using a pneumatic tube system rather than tills) and, finally, Barkers in 2006. It was the end of an era for Kensington. For the last quarter of the nineteenth century and for much of the twentieth, these were the names that drew consumers in their millions. As the dazzled 'Woman Correspondent' of the *Nottingham Journal* put it in 1956, Kensington really was an 'Aladdin's Cave of shopping'.

These days much of the upper floors are occupied by the *Daily Mail* newspaper group and the *Evening Standard*, while the ground floor is home to the American Whole Foods Market's flagship London store.

DERRY & TOMS 99 Kensington High Street, W8 • 1862–1973

While the racier, more fashion-conscious Suffragettes favoured Selfridge's rooftop restaurant as a meeting place (Gordon Selfridge flew the purple, white and green flag whenever Mrs Pankhurst emerged from jail), Derry & Toms' tea room was the favoured spot for the non-militant suffragists in their more sober, practical attire. In other words, middle-class bluestockings shopped at Derry & Toms; upper-class It girls favoured Selfridges.

But no-one could afford to ignore the coming generation, and this venerable department store – far older than Barkers, its roots going back to the Toms family grocery of 1826 – had always moved astutely with the times. In 1911, it was advertising 'Charming Hats

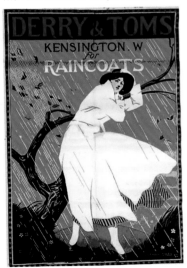

for the June 17th Demonstration' in the *Suffragette* newspaper. 'Special Display at Derry & Toms, Kensington High St.' The Women's Coronation Procession, organised by Mrs Pankhurst's WSPU, attracted 40,000 marching women. In 1913, next to a

full-page *Suffragette* article reporting 'A Triumphant Year! Great Increase in Subscriptions', Derry & Toms took a full-page advertisement for a 'Carbonide' fur safe, 'A Wonderful Invention for the safe-keeping of furs at home'.

Tactical reinvention was the name of the game. Acquired by Barkers after the Great War, Derry & Toms had its greatest moment for reinvention in 1929–33 with its Art Deco rebuild. The pressing need

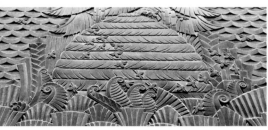

for street widening gave the perfect opportunity to create a thoroughly modern department store for a new era. Bernard George's design soared six floors high, a bold and simple building with a fine stone façade of columns and friezes. Beautiful aluminium animals by the sculptor Walter Gilbert decorated the exterior, along with stone panel reliefs of 'Labour and Technology' by C. J. Mabey.

A Garden in the Sky ...

One of the world's wonders—the unique Derry Roof Gardens—
some 1½ acres, 100 ft. above ground level, with green lawns,
shady trees; a flowing stream and waterfall; and several distinct
types of garden (such as the Tudor and Spanish Gardens) which
are perfect examples of their kind. Open during the fine weather
months in aid of charity. Lunches, teas and refreshments in the
Sun Restaurant.

Visitors to London
Welcome to Kensington

LONDON'S FINEST SHOPPING CENTRE

BARKERS, DERRYS and PONTINGS welcome you to the historic and
beautiful district of Kensington. These three great stores, whose gracious
buildings dominate the main thoroughfare, offer a shopping service which, in
the opinion of many, is unequalled in the Kingdom.

TAX-FREE SHOPPING
for OVERSEAS VISITORS
who may buy free of purchase
tax under the Personal Export
Scheme (and the Coupon Scheme
for U.S.A. & Canada) including
specially reserved goods.
Enquire for the Export Bureau.

Six Restaurants. Buses from all districts. Underground to Kensington High Street Stn. (Inner Circle).
B.E.A. Air Station almost opposite. (A few minutes from Earl's Court and Olympia Exhibitions).

Derrys | **BARKERS** OF KENSINGTON | **Pontings**

KENSINGTON HIGH STREET. LONDON. W.8

Five hundred trees and a flock of flamingos

The Derry & Toms roof garden was the vision of Barkers'
MD Trevor Bowen, keen to bring some New York dazzle to
Kensington. He commissioned the Welsh landscape architect
Ralph Hancock, who'd just designed the eleventh-floor
'Garden of the Nations' in 1935 for New York's Rockefeller
Centre.

Work began in the summer of 1936. One and half acres of soil
was hauled up to the rooftop and installed at a depth of two

and half feet, along with a drainage bed of bricks and clinker.
Water for the flowing stream and fountains was pumped from
the store's artesian well, 500 feet below the High Street. Five

Tellingly, a Chicago architect, C. A. Wheeler,
was hired to create the ultimate interior in the
'horizontal' American style: open plan, separate
floors, no fire hazard central staircases. A battery of
eight lifts in onyx and black marble shot shoppers to
the upper floors – particularly to the greatest draw
of all, the Rainbow Room on the fifth floor. Lit by a
long, elliptical skylight and concealed neon lighting,
this restaurant adjoined a fashion theatre with an

equally cool, elegant layout. The suave restraint
of the interior, with its concealed lighting (not an
electric bulb in sight), walnut furniture and blue
and gold carpets, brought Derry & Toms renown as
a classic of English Art Deco. In the words of one
professor of architecture, the new store had 'spirit
and sparkle'.

Here, finally, was competition for Selfridges.
Among the thousands of curious onlookers at its

hundred varieties of tree and shrubs were planted, including alpine species from Pennsylvania, thought to be best suited to the London weather. There was a sun pavilion, an English woodland garden, a Spanish garden, a Tudor garden and a flock of flamingos. Bowen had wanted a sense of enchantment, a refuge from the din 100 feet below, and his vision succeeded. A local vicar is said to have sought out its tranquil haven every day for thirteen years in order to write his sermons.

'Derry Gardens' opened to great excitement in 1938, but one name was left out of the story. The previous year, Ralph Hancock had been approached by an ambitious young plantswoman, who had seen his garden at the 1937 Chelsea

Flower Show. Hancock offered Esme Williams 10 shillings a week to come and work for him. Esme was responsible for much, if not all the planting.

Esme Bradburne (her married name), who died in 2000, remembered the roof garden project in detail – including the 38,000 bedding plants and 15,000 bulbs she planted herself. She recalled how stone from Pennsylvania was brought

Esme Bradburne.

in as it coped better with London pollution, and how she had personally 'liberated' Thames stones for use in the little stream which ran through the English woodland garden. In 1946 she became one of founder members of the Soil Association.

opening, at 2.30 p.m. on Thursday, 30 March 1933, rival store chiefs Gordon Selfridge, Austin Reed and Eric Gamage were spotted. The *Daily Mail* thought it a 'dream palace' for 'the coming generation'; the *Daily Mirror* was quick to notice that 'while the premises are luxurious', those with 'depleted purses' could afford the prices. Even the discreet lighting in the men's and ladies' lavatories got a write-up in the *Architect & Building News*.

House of Fraser's closure of the store in 1973 saw Big Biba move in and take maximum advantage of the building's Art Deco opulence. The roof garden (100 of whose trees now have preservation orders) later became a nightclub run by Richard Branson's Virgin group, but has been closed since 2018.

BIG BIBA 99 Kensington High Street, W8 (formerly Derry & Toms) • 1973-75

The opening of Big Biba in the old Derry & Toms building on Kensington High Street was one of the most anticipated retail events of the twentieth century. It was the first big store opening since the Second World War, exciting the press as much as the opening of Selfridges in 1909. The papers dubbed it the 'Superstore Boutique'. Anyone who visited Big Biba remembered it. The *Sunday Times*, observing the last rites in 1975, called it 'the most beautiful store in the world'.

In 1969, when the fashion label Biba moved from cramped premises on Kensington Church Street to a store on Kensington High Street, founder-designer Barbara Hulanicki found herself intrigued by her neighbour, Derry & Toms. 'It was so beautiful and so unappreciated. No one there had any respect for the building or its superb detail.' Many of its assistants, Hulanicki reckoned, had been working there 'since its opening day and were now over sixty'. Biba's manifesto was one of youth. How could she get her hands on that store?

Learning in 1973 of House of Fraser's decision to sell it, Hulanicki and her husband Stephen Fitz-Simon persuaded their backers, Dorothy Perkins, to acquire the property. They had just 12 weeks to transform the store, and they started by revealing the building's original Art Deco bones.

Big Biba set out to evoke the Golden Age of Hollywood – with antiques, with 20,000 mottled mirrors, with potted palms and ostrich feathers. 'A palace of apricot marble, coloured counters and fake leopard-skin walls', was how *Vogue* summed it up on opening day, Monday, 10 September 1973; 'seven

Ready Steady Go! presenter Cathy McGowan and singer Cilla Black lead the way into the original Biba Boutique in Kensington Church Street, February 1966.

Twiggy sits alone in the Rainbow Room of Biba's High Street Kensington store, 1973.

floors of fantasy.' *Good Housekeeping* invited readers to 'blame Barbara if you can't hear yourself shop for the heavy rock music . . . if you can't see whether a dress is black, brown or navy because you're shopping in semi-darkness.'

There were Biba cosmetics, Biba home wares,

children's clothes, sportswear, furniture, paint, wallpaper, stationery. There was even a Biba bookshop specialising in art and design. Household goods were elevated to art, causing the *Financial Times* to sniff that 'the joke has been taken too far. One bright pink nylon broom is fun, but a barrowful is a little worrying.'

As with those great American department stores

of the early twentieth century, fantasy had been given free rein. The children's floor had a storybook village with toadstool tables. A giant record player dominated the music department. Up on the roof garden, fibreglass Bambis jostled with straw peacock chairs. On the fashion floor, shoppers rarely bothered with the changing rooms. The Rainbow Room was a restaurant, concert venue and celebrity hang-out all in one for the likes of Mick Jagger and Julie Christie.

Biba shop assistants were a breed apart, coming out from behind the counter and communing with the customers – who, in turn, treated the place like home. This was the first store to let people try on make-up before buying. Girls would arrive bare faced on the way to work, and leave, freshly made up.

To conservative Kensington residents, the store windows were a travesty. Brown and gold sofas stretched the entire plate-glass length, harbouring sleeping tramps, ladies from the suburbs, office girls eating their lunch and the odd priest. 'These spoke more loudly of Biba than any display of stiff dummies would,' claimed Hulanicki. 'Did the public need to be reassured by pretentious fibreglass figures in contortionist poses that gleamed false smiles at them to lure them into the store? We thought not.'

Their new financial backers, British Land, thought otherwise.

After barely a year of operations, an embittered Hulanicki and Fitz-Simon lost creative control. Despite attracting over a million visitors a week, the building proved a more valuable asset than the business it generated. The store was closed in September 1975 and the building sold off.

The Biba brand was reincarnated, without Hulanicki, in 2007–8 with designs by Bella Freud, and by House of Fraser in 2009 using a team led by Hector Castro. But nothing ever quite dazzled like the original. The building is now home to a Marks & Spencer, a GAP store, H&M, Sony Music offices and a gym.

PONTINGS 123–127 Kensington High Street, W8 · 1873–1970

As you walk through the shopping arcade towards High Street Kensington Underground station, take a look to your right. Those arched display windows are all that remains of Pontings – 'the House for Value', as it became known. Ironically, it was the expense of developing the western side of Kensington Arcade that took the original Pontings into liquidation in 1907.

Once 'the largest retail and fancy goods and silk business in London', Pontings was the greatest rival of its next-door-but-one neighbour Barkers. Started by four West Country brothers, the firm acquired a seventeenth-century mansion, Scarsdale House, former home to the Curzon family and known to contain a haunted room associated with a murder (pulled down in 1899 to make way for 'an up-to-date tea and retiring room for customers').

Pontings' speciality was 'art needlework' supplies, that time-killing pastime of the Victorian lady, with an in-house 'school of needlework' cannily creating a demand for the store's own goods. In 1899, at its zenith, Pontings commissioned the architect Arthur Sykes to design a grand new premises – a six-floor Italianate palazzo. But by the time it was finished in 1901, debts were mounting. With no more Ponting brothers at the helm, the company was in trouble.

It was the moment for John Barker to scoop Pontings into his net. On 30 April 1907, the *Evening News* reported 'remarkable scenes' in Kensington High Street when 'hundreds of shoppers made a determined raid on the shop lately occupied by Messrs Ponting Brothers, drapers.' Having acquired it for a knock-down £84,000, John Barker & Co were 'selling the entire stock . . . at immense reductions'. The commissionaires 'did their utmost to stem the crowds',

Pontings didn't escape the Suffragette window-smashing spree of 4 March 1912.

but were 'absolutely helpless before the onslaught'. When those determined Edwardian women forced the heavy doors open, the 500 assistants inside were 'simply swamped'.

The police were called in as reinforcements. John Barker was taking no chances: two months earlier, rallied by Emmeline Pankhurst's slogan 'Deeds Not

'Pontings proved that there was a working class in the vicinity, and they *did* need to buy stuff.'
The London Wanderer blog

High Street, Kensington, W. No. 3535.

Words', hundreds of Suffragettes had stormed Parliament, smashing windows and chaining themselves to railings. One woman at the Pontings sale scrum assured a reporter they were 'not intent on any wrecking expedition', but 'simply after bargains'.

Nevertheless, Royal Kensington sighed with relief when it was all over. Five years later, the store got its own windows smashed by a wave of militant Suffragettes.

The new Pontings was all about bargains. 'THE HOUSE FOR VALUE' went up in huge letters over that elegant façade, and the thriftier classes were courted hard. By the Fifties, Barkers' Sales Specials were shunting shoppers into town by train. Station placards promised a journey 'From Door to Store'; lunch on board was free.

When Pontings fell victim to House of Fraser's rationalisation in 1970, the name briefly lived on. All the unsold stock from the closing-down sale was transferred to Barkers' own lower ground floor, renamed 'Pontings Bargain Basement'. The great bonanza lasted four years, and is remembered to this day. The old Pontings building was pulled down in 1976, but you can still catch a glimpse of those remaining store windows on your way to and from the Tube.

The Department Store's Slow Decline

It's estimated that an astonishing 83 per cent of Britain's remaining department stores have closed since 2016. These include whole chains, like Debenhams, Beales, and much of House of Fraser, as well as old-established and cherished independents such as Boswells of Oxford, trading since 1738 and the second-oldest department store in the world.

But, in truth, department stores have been closing for years, decades – indeed, since before the last war. It's just that the reasons have changed, and the pace, of late, has speeded up.

The latest wave of casualties have fallen victim to two years of pandemic lockdown. Even the *grande dame* of the high street, John Lewis, was compelled to withdraw from the centre of cities as major as Birmingham and Sheffield. But the closures of previous eras mark other, wider social forces. For London, it was the gradual creep of the metropolis. Even as late as the Sixties, places like Croydon and Sutton were separate towns in their own right: Surrey towns, each with their own home-grown department stores. But nowadays, anywhere within the Travelcard zone is really London, and all railway lines lead to the centre.

Also, by the Sixties, young women had stopped shopping like their mothers. Those department stores that stubbornly ignored the swinging Sixties and psychedelic Seventies were left in the mothballs. Young house model Julia Gregson cringed at the 'utterly dreary' tweed suits she had to show off for Debenham & Freebody in 1966, making her look 'absolutely ancient'. You ignored the coming generation at your peril.

By the Seventies, property speculation was on the march: many buildings were suddenly worth more for their real estate. In 1972, Gamages of Holborn – still a busy

Bluewater: a generic shopping-mall with no connection to family, place or past.

Boswells of Oxford, trading since 1738, closed its doors in 2020.

Lakeside, Bluewater, Westfield White City, Westfield Stratford – these are the names that now roll off consumers' tongues; names dreamed up by marketeers for mega-malls with no connection to family, place or past.

But both the shopping mall and the high street are struggling to compete with the meteoric rise of online shopping. Now permanently institutionalised by the pandemic, it accounts for 30 per cent of all sales in the UK. The Internet is the new department store in town – and on a worldwide scale. This is where we now go for a ball of wool, a new kettle or washing machine, or a swimsuit in *that* brand, *that* colour and *that* size.

and profitable store – was shut and levelled to make way for a mirror-glass office tower. 'Oh, unimaginable horror!' wrote the novelist Barbara Pym in her diary, on learning of its fate. Hundreds of 'lunchtime idlers and browsers' like herself would, she predicted, be left 'desolate'. And so they were.

Then came the out-of-town shopping centre, a novelty destination in itself with, crucially, free parking.

'How quickly these palaces of consumption have reached their sell-by date.' – Janet Street-Porter

'Department stores are far more than shops. Their closure feels like losing a park, a library, an arts or leisure centre. Every town mourns these lost urban sitting rooms.' – Polly Toynbee

The Survivors and the Future

'In the future', Andy Warhol once observed, deadpan, 'all department stores will become museums and all museums will become department stores.' And why not? There's an obvious parallel between galleries and stores, both offering up sumptuous or curious objects to be marvelled at.

In 1928, many thousands were drawn to two groundbreaking exhibitions of modern art and interiors at Shoolbreds and neighbouring Waring & Gillow. For a brief moment in time, these progressive department

stores really *were* the greatest museums in town. At Gamages, generations of children learned to really *look*, critically, as they assessed tier upon tier of toys and gadgetry on display. Kennards of Croydon held Wild West shows on its roof; Chiesmans of Lewisham pulled in the crowds with its vicious lion, Vixen.

In today's climate, only the fittest will survive. London's remaining great department stores have tapped back into the golden age of showmanship, when Marshall & Snelgrove or Derry & Toms really were the

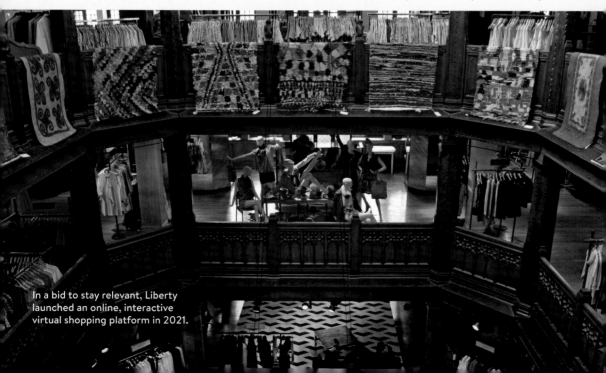

In a bid to stay relevant, Liberty launched an online, interactive virtual shopping platform in 2021.

176

most modern, lavish and breathtaking destinations, selling dazzle and dreams along with the drapery. Selfridges has pioneered the change – just as it did at its opening in 1909. Creative director Alannah Weston ushered in artists and gave them free reign – in the store windows, in the 'Ultralounge' exhibition space, on the shop floor. She took Selfridges back to its Edwardian founder's roots, with the belief that retail should be *theatre*. 'I want people to leave with a smile on their face'. Where Selfridges led, others followed – Harrods, Fortnum & Mason, Liberty and Harvey Nichols.

We're at a pivotal moment. Department stores are no longer how we instinctively shop, as our parents once did. And yet, designed to impress and inspire, they make up some of the finest and most significant buildings on London's streets – indeed, on high streets throughout Britain. With imaginative re-use, there's no reason why these landmark buildings shouldn't come back to life again.

The Art Deco RACS store on Lewisham High Street was saved from the wrecking ball and converted into sleekly elegant flats. Randalls of Uxbridge has received a similar, sensitive treatment, its modestly Modernist façade beautifully restored. Residents of Battersea are tentatively embracing the new-look Arding & Hobbs, with its wavy roofline and mixed-use spaces. In Brixton, the edifice built in 1906 to house Bon Marché's staff has been named 'The Department Store' in a wink at the past, playing on its groovy, new, mixed-use incarnation. No matter that none of its punters have likely set foot in one: they're gathering, animatedly,

The Department Store, Bon Marché's former staff accommodation in Brixton, now hosts a restaurant, a workspace and the architectural practice that redesigned the building.

over food and beverages, much like an emporium's soda bar of old.

BARBERS 417-429 North End Road, Fulham, SW6 • 1891-1994

'Woman Pushed Through Plate Glass Window' ran the headline. 'Killed When Car Dashes Onto Pavement In Effort to Avoid Collision.' The plate glass window was Barbers'.

Ellen Emms, the 24-year-old wife of a gas fitter, was making her way home on Thursday 15 March, 1928, when a car suddenly mounted the kerb on the corner of Armadale Road and crashed through Barber's window, carrying her with it. Ellen died that afternoon in Fulham Hospital from shock and multiple injuries.

Oddly, the name 'Barbers' wasn't mentioned in  reports of the inquest and subsequent trial of driver Alfred Priddle. This was because the department store's 60-year-old owner, Yorkshireman Fred Holgate Barber, had just been made Mayor of Fulham. Mrs Barber, the new mayoress, was 'a lady of charming personality who has always taken a keen interest in the welfare of Fulham.'

Barbers wasn't an enormous store, or a particularly grand store. But since its small beginnings in 1891, it had become central to its local community. While other, larger emporiums struggled to stay relevant into the Sixties and beyond, Barbers never lost touch with its customers – most of which were known by name to staff.

In 1965 we find Fred Barber's grandson in the

Kensington Gazette: suave, black-haired Graham Barber, MD, handing over a prize Automatic 90 Electrolux Cleaner to 'attractive, blonde housewife, Mrs M. Rooney, of Comeragh Road, West Kensington.'.

North End Road was not a wealthy demographic. Bargains mattered, and consumer temptations could prove overwhelming. In 1969 a 70-year-old housewife, Mrs Eva Louisa Perry, 'was accused at West London of stealing a hat, valued at £1.10s., from Barber's Store, Fulham. The elderly housewife was remanded on bail.' Shoplifters among Barbers' aspirational customers were common.

When Janet Street-Porter was growing up in London Barbers still had the Lamson pneumatic system for transferring cash around the store (see pp. 84-6). 'Where did these tubes go?' she wondered in her 2004 memoir, *Baggage*. 'Mum would never tell me. I imagined a grotto, like Santa's, under the store full of clerks in black suits with starchy white collars sitting at long desks counting out money and issuing receipts, a bit like something out of a Charles Dickens novel.'

Barbers expanded in 1979, promising the very latest in soft furnishings: 'Readymade stretch lounge suite covers. What a practical and economical way to give a new look to your lounge!' Not forgetting net curtains – 'often sadly neglected in soft furnishings departments, but not at Barbers, whose net department is one of the best in London. No home is complete without them.'

By 1988, however, yet another 'modern' refurbishment smacked slightly of desperation. Out went the polished green linoleum and the old wooden

staircase. Three air-conditioned floors were unveiled, fully carpeted; they'd even installed (rather late in the day) a lift. Brand names 'you'd normally expect to trek to the West End to find' included Christian Dior, Triumph and Wolford. But it was too late. Barbers now seemed hopelessly old-fashioned. Even the new floor plan couldn't conceal its true identity – 'On the first floor you'll find the Chiropodist next to Knitting Yarns.'

Graham Barber placed a heartfelt letter in the local press in August 1994, thanking customers. 'Successive generations of the Barber family have been delighted to have been of service to the people of Fulham, ably supported by all staff.' After 102 years of trading, North End Road's favourite store closed its doors.

The Barbers building still exists, today housing Sports Direct and a bank.

RANDALLS Vine Street, Uxbridge, UB8 • 1891-2015

'It's up there with bereavement,' said Sir John Randall, on having to close the family business after 123 years continuous trading. The Uxbridge and South Ruislip MP was the fourth generation to have worked here;

his two sons were the fifth and last. Randalls' twenty-first-century decline was obvious to anyone walking down Vine Street in Uxbridge. By 2015, only five of the distinctive red neon letters on its Modernist facade lit up: 'RA - - - LLS'. It wasn't a good omen.

What Randalls did have, to the end, was period appeal. It was a near-perfect 1930s time capsule in every detail, from the two-storey exterior (brick faced in cream faience with Royal Doulton Carraraware detailing) to the interior (original cash desk and signage, a pneumatic tube system and structural columns

surrounded by cast iron radiators). Given its proximity to Pinewood Studios, the department store popped up regularly in film and TV – from *Dixon of Dock Green* in the 1950s, to the more recent *Only Fools and Horses*, *Endeavour* and *New Tricks*. Post-closure, Randalls' exterior made a fleeting appearance in the 2017 period film *Goodbye Christopher Robin*, for its almost continuous run of plate glass windows set in fluted bronze frames.

Sir John's great-grandfather Philip founded the homeware and furnishings store in 1891, buying up an

existing shop on Vine Street and renaming it. By the time of Philip's death in 1936, his son Bert was running the store and keen to put down his marker in this

burgeoning London suburb. He commissioned a local elder, architect William Eves of Uxbridge High Street, to create something splendidly new. Eves could never have imagined that his modestly Modernist store with its off-centre tower would be Grade II-listed (2008), a label that saved it from the developers' bulldozers in 2019, when Randalls' big Sixties extension was demolished.

Randalls has been saved, restored and is now the groovy period face of a block of contemporary apartments, released in January 2022 with a blaze of publicity. The original building has been renamed 'Gatsby House', and original elements from the interiors have been retained in an attempt to 'respectfully pay homage to the history of the building'.

BRADLEYS 1 Chepstow Place, W11 • 1870 - 1952

oday, a two bedroom flat up in these attics will set you back £1.6m – the spot where 'Bradleys' Young Ladies' once slept packed like sardines in dormitories, confined by the loathed 'living in' system. Bradleys' young ladies were renowned throughout London for their manners, smart appearance and discreet ministrations – for this was no ordinary department store.

It started simply as a cold store for furs in the 1860s, but by 1912 Bradley & Sons Arctic Fur Store was Europe's biggest fur specialist; the house where every item was priced in guineas (anything up to 2,000 guineas – around £100,000 today). To old and new wealth alike, this proved an irresistible affectation.

Founder Samuel Bradley began on the ground in Canada and Russia, importing raw fur skins by buying direct from trappers. Sable, ermine, silver fox, lynx, seal, musquash, beaver, mink and mole... By the 1920s, in the hands of his sons, the store had its own in-house fashion designers and a reputation not only for furs but tailoring, dress-making, millinery and motoring fashions.

By the 1930s, when clients included Winston and Clementine Churchill, Queen Mary and Hollywood starlets, the store underwent a sumptuous Arts Deco interior refit. (It was felt that the imposing exterior, designed in 1905 by J. E. Stubbs, couldn't be bettered). A fleet of six Chrysler cars was commissioned for use as a free taxi service for its customers. Bradleys could also look after a client's entire wardrobe season by season, overseeing cleaning, repairs and alterations.

In 1936, at the height of the abdication crisis, Mrs Winston Churchill paid £2/8s (around £160) to have a white ermine collar and cuffs cleaned on a white, fur-lined coat. The following year, during the Hitler appeasement row, she paid £3/9s for the storage of furs, and the renovation of a black velvet evening coat trimmed with white ermine.

Bradleys ministered to thousands. Daily, some 200 women might come in for fittings (Queen Mary

The Exclusiveness of Bradley Furs

The Bradley model wrap illustrated here is in fine quality Natural Mink.

The distinguished fur models designed by Bradley furriers can be seen only in the Bradley Salons. They cannot be reproduced by any other House. In addition to their exclusiveness, they represent the finest possible value in fine furs because they are actually manufactured by Bradleys on the premises at Chepstow Place, thereby eliminating all intermediate profits. You are cordially invited to inspect the Winter Collection which is now being shown daily in the Salons; or if that is impossible, a brochure illustrating 86 of the new models will be gladly sent on request.

Bradleys
CHEPSTOW PLACE W2
BAYswater 1200

had her own fitting room). The store employed 1,500 staff, housing its workers first in the attics, then in segregated hostels nearby. 'Badleys' Young Ladies' were eventually rewarded with a large, Art Deco-style hostel in 1936 - Bowden Court, still a hostel today on 24 Ladbroke Road, designed by the store's interior architect J. A. Bowden.

Requisitioned during the Second World War as a First Aid Post, Bradleys suffered in the pinched, post-war years. It was sold to the Co-operative Insurance Company in 1952, the building renamed 'Baynards House' and occupied by several grey government ministries over the coming years. The Bradley's brand was acquired in 1953 by the Debenhams Group, re-opening as furriers in the West End next to Debenham & Freebody. Meanwhile, the Bradley family pivoted to become specialist dry cleaners.

1 Chepstow Place opened in 2000 as a 'prestigious, portered block' known as The Baynards. The Deco interiors by architect John Dean Monroe Harvey are long gone, but the verdigris 'B' cartouches on the façade remain. Look up, as you enter Space NK and other shops at pavement level.

WHITELEYS   31 Westbourne Grove, then 151 Queensway, W2 • 1863–1981

In the last week of the January sales, 1907, William Whiteley was shot dead in his own department store by a man claiming to be his illegitimate son. Horace Rayner killed the 75-year-old retail impresario at point-

blank range as he stood by the umbrella counter: two bullets in the head from a Colt revolver. The gunman then tried and failed to take his own life.

'Sensational Murder in Westbourne Grove', ran the headline in the *Illustrated Police News*. William Whiteley, self-made millionaire, earned many enemies in his long career. 'Someone has an animus against me,' he uttered in 1887, after an immense shop fire reduced his store to ashes. When the flames were finally put out, by no fewer than 34 of London's total of 45 steam fire engines, he offered

a £2,000 reward for information, a huge sum in those days. Whiteley was right to be suspicious: that decade his department store was torched six times in five years.

A squat, bewhiskered, bull-like Yorkshireman, William Whiteley had abundant energy, a huge ego and an unerring gift for self-publicity. He was also an aggressive litigant and a punitive employer, with

> Henry Higgins: 'Where does one buy a lady's frock?'
> Colonel Pickering: 'Whiteleys, of course.'
> Lerner and Loewe, *My Fair Lady*

Westbourne Grove in 1890 – by which time Whiteleys employed 6000 staff, most living in male and female dormitories nearby.

a personality best reflected in his choice of pet, a champion English bulldog called King Orry. His Bayswater store was dubbed the 'Universal Provider', with the boast that it could supply 'everything from an elephant to a pin'. When a customer bet that he couldn't get him an elephant, Whiteley hired one from a circus and delivered it within four hours.

This was the first privately owned retail establishment in London to become a fully-fledged department store – a store that impressed even the Americans. In 1876, the *New York Daily Graphic* was amazed by its rapid growth: 'Mr Whiteley will take charge of you from cradle to the grave and give you your meals as go along – if you can pay for it.' Mark Twain, arriving in London in 1908, used Whiteleys to rent him an English country house with servants.

Born the son of a Yorkshire corn dealer, William Whiteley had his eureka moment on a visit to the

The Rotunda restaurant, loved by literati.

Great Exhibition in London in 1851. Six million visitors viewed this vast display of British and international merchandise. Many returned to the capital to try their luck. Whiteley finished his draper's apprenticeship, saved up £700, and opened his first Fancy Goods shop on Westbourne Grove, aged 31 (soon to marry his shop girl, Harriet Hill). The year was 1863: London's first underground steam railway line, the Metropolitan, had just opened in nearby Edgware Road.

Whiteley's stock was not unusual, but his methods for the time were. To achieve high turnover on low margins, he simply undercut the competition. 'I knew a good article when I saw it,' he later said, when the *Pall Mall Gazette* asked him the secret to his success. He also claimed to have 'inexhaustible energy and business pluck.' Before the nineteenth century was out, Whiteley's had colonised over 20 neighbouring properties in Westbourne Grove and around the corner in Queen's Road (now Queensway).

The temperament driving this dizzying expansion was an obsessive one. Whiteley patrolled his establishment 'like a roaring lion', and was intensely disliked and feared by his staff. By 1890 over 6,000 were employed in the business, most of them living in-house in dormitories and working 7 a.m. to 11 p.m., six days a week. The 176 'Rules of W. Whiteley's Establishment' were much hated, covering everything from staff dress, to correct treatment of customers, to the handling of money. Any infringement, however petty, would result in a fine of sixpence. The beneficiary of these fines was William Whiteley himself.

But the man could also be charm itself, standing outside the shop entrance with his deferential smile, 'bowing to the right and left quite in the grand forgotten style', as the *Daily Chronicle* noted. He personally welcomed some of the great beauties of the day – the actress Lily Langtry (mistress of the Prince of Wales), Alexandra, Princess of Wales and Queen Victoria's youngest child, Princess Beatrice. His greatest coup was furnishing a minor royal wedding at Buckingham Palace in 1896, thrilling the elderly Queen so much that she granted an unsolicited Royal Warrant.

Ultimately, Whiteley's wealth and libido cost him his life. It was never proven whether 29-year-old Horace Rayner was or wasn't the proprietor's illegitimate son, but his evidence at the Old Bailey solicited much public sympathy. His death sentence was commuted after a petition, and he served just 12 years in prison. Later that year, both victim and gunman became waxworks at Madame Tussaud's. William Whiteley's posthumous reputation was severely damaged by the revelation of a string of extra-marital affairs. He left £1 million in his will, around £100 million today.

In 1911, with two sons at the helm, the business relocated to a grand new store in Queensway, designed in Portland stone by Belcher and Joass. The 'largest shop in the world' now had a theatre and a mini golf course on the roof. Here, under the elegant dome of the Cupola restaurant, the Edwardian literati would meet for lunch: Conrad, Chesterton, Galsworthy, Belloc *et al.* The 'Harrods of Bayswater' became a twentieth-century institution to a certain sort of west London woman, supplying them with every household

need, drawing them on frequent visits (as much of inspection as of purchase) and providing material for endless gossip in an age before celebrity magazines and soap operas. The writer Osbert Lancaster's Aunt Jenny viewed Whiteley's 'as part of her domestic domain'.

After several changes of ownership, including acquisition by its great rival Selfridges in 1927, Whiteleys finally closed as a department store in 1981. It then became a shopping mall, but the opening of Westfield in Shepherd's Bush severely dented its trade. The building is now being developed as 'The Whiteley' – an upmarket blend of retail, cinema, apartments and a hotel.

A West End Lost Department Stores Walk

This 1.5-mile walk from Selfridges to the former Simpsons takes you past more than ten of the capital's department stores that are no longer with us – and three that are. It is best appreciated on a quiet Sunday morning when the crowds and traffic are at a minimum.

Start: BOND STREET TUBE
Finish: PICCADILLY CIRCUS TUBE

Exit Bond Street Tube through the partly subterranean West One shopping centre (to experience one of the more unappealing examples of the modern retail environment) onto Oxford Street, cross over and turn left, walking westwards to the huge, classically pillared frontage of **Selfridges**, topped by its row of fluttering flags.

Then double back eastwards along Oxford Street back past the Tube station, past the fine black granite Art Deco frontage of what used to be HMV's flagship music store and is now Candy World, one of the street's recent infestation of candy stores. Opposite Woodstock Street is what used to be **Debenhams**, and – even earlier – **Marshall & Snelgrove**, now being converted for office and retail use.

Turn left along the former store's left-hand side up Marylebone Lane, and follow this up to the Cock & Lion pub on Wigmore Street. Turn right and, from the corner of Welbeck Street on the south side, opposite the Wigmore Hall, is the former **Debenham & Freebody**, its ground floor now housing furniture showrooms and a branch of Boots.

Turn right down Wimpole Street to reach on your left the interwar bulk of the former **House of Fraser**, previously **D. H. Evans**, awaiting repurposing.

Turn left along Henrietta Place and right down Old Cavendish Street alongside **John Lewis**, still very much open, and turn left back onto Oxford Street, stopping to look up at Barbara Hepworth's winged figure on the store's eastern corner. Continue past the Sixties building of the former British Home Stores (never quite a department store) and cross over Oxford Circus.

Opposite on the north-east corner of Oxford Circus is the former **Peter Robinson**, the corner now a booming branch of Niketown, the rest recently vacated by TopShop and soon to be taken over by IKEA.

Continue eastwards on the north side of Oxford Street. Between Great Titchfield Street and Winsley Street is the Edwardian red-brick that used to be **Waring & Gillow**, now H&M and Uniqlo, almost opposite the black granite Art Deco of M&S's Pantheon store.

At Wells Street you come upon the early Art Deco of what used to be **Bourne & Hollingsworth**, with a gold winged statue above the portico. Now it's a branch of Next flanked by Gap and O₂.

Cross over Oxford Street and return along the south side as far as Argyll Street, where you turn left. Opposite the London Palladium is the Portland stone of what was **Dickins & Jones**. Turn right along Little Argyll Street and then left onto Regent Street past the front of the former store, now a succession of clothing chains.

Cross over Great Marlborough Street, noting the mock-half-timbered frontage of **Liberty** to your left, still happily in business, and continue down as far as Hamleys. This was previously **Swears & Wells**, and before that **Galeries Lafayette**. Further down, the brown marble façade beyond Tenison Court used to be **Robinson & Cleaver** and is now Calvin Klein and Massimo Dutti.

Cross over Regent Street and follow it down to Piccadilly Circus (with Tube station for your homeward journey), bearing right, past what used to be **Swan & Edgar** on the corner site, into Piccadilly. Eighty yards along on the opposite side is the flagship of the Waterstones bookshop chain, that used to be (as the gold lettering still proclaims) **Simpson Piccadilly**, its curvaceous Moderne interior of cream marble largely untouched, where you'll be able to buy more copies of the book you hold in your hand.

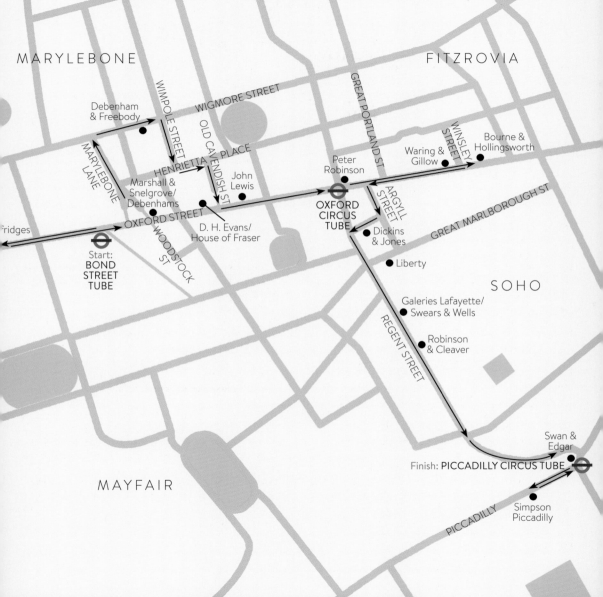

MARYLEBONE

FITZROVIA

Debenham & Freebody

WIMPOLE STREET

WIGMORE STREET

GREAT PORTLAND ST

OLD CAVENDISH ST

HENRIETTA PLACE

MARYLEBONE LANE

Marshall & Snelgrove/ Debenhams

John Lewis

Peter Robinson

WINSLEY STREET

Waring & Gillow

Bourne & Hollingsworth

OXFORD CIRCUS TUBE

ARGYLL STREET

~fridges

OXFORD STREET

WOODSTOCK ST

D. H. Evans/ House of Fraser

GREAT MARLBOROUGH ST

Start: BOND STREET TUBE

Dickins & Jones

Liberty

SOHO

Galeries Lafayette/ Swears & Wells

REGENT STREET

Robinson & Cleaver

MAYFAIR

Swan & Edgar

Finish: PICCADILLY CIRCUS TUBE

Simpson Piccadilly

PICCADILLY

A Lost Department Store Chronology

1812 – 1949	Stagg & Mantle
1812 – 1982	Swan & Edgar
1813 – 1975	Debenham & Freebody
1816 – 1970	Swears & Wells
1817 – 1934	Shoolbreds
1833 – 1975	Marshall & Snelgrove
1833 – 1974	Peter Robinson
1835 – 2006	Dickins & Jones
1840 – 1968	Jeremiah Rotherham & Co
1850 – 1990	Pratts
1850s – 1969	Wickhams
1853 – 1973	Kennards
1858 – 1968	Gorringes
1862 – 2012	Allders
1862 – 1973	Derry & Toms
1863 – 1981	Whiteleys
1866 – 1982	The Civil Service Supply Association
1866 – 1931	The Civil Service Cooperative Society
1867 – 1990	Jones Brothers
1867 – 1980	Jones & Higgins
1868 – 1985	The Royal Arsenal Co-operative Society (RACS)
1869 – 1967	Woollands
1870 – 2006	Barkers
1870 – 1952	Bradleys
1870 – 1975	J. R. Roberts
1871 – 2022	Army & Navy
1873 – 1970	Pontings
1877 – 1975	Bon Marché
1877 – 1985	Grants
1878 – 2001	D. H. Evans
1878 – 1972	Gamages
1880 – 1920	Junior Army & Navy
1880 – 1941	Quin & Axtens
1882 – 1949	Holdrons
1884 – 2020	Arding & Hobbs
1884 – 1997	Chiesmans
1890 – 2018	Bodgers
1891 – 1994	Barbers
1891 – 2015	Randalls
1894 – 1984	Robinson & Cleaver
1898 – 1983	Bearmans
1899 – 1992	Shinners
1900 – 1981	John Barnes
1902 – 1983	Bourne & Hollingsworth
1902 – 2010	Harrison Gibson
1903 – 1980	Waring & Gillow
1908 – 1937	Drages
1920 – 1972	Galeries Lafayette
1936 – 1999	Simpson Piccadilly
1937 – 1963	Daniel Neal & Sons
1973 – 1975	Big Biba

Index

Picture credits

© London Metropolitan Archives: 2–3, 23 (left), 87, 141, 161 (right), 185, 186 (top) Private Collection: 4–5, 46 (left), 47 (left)

Getty Images: 10, 11, 64 (left), 72–3, 82, 85, 101, 116(bottom), 117, 140 (left), 143, 151 (bottom left), 156 (bottom), 167–9

Mary Evans: 12, 13, 14, 15 (top), 17 (bottom), 18, 19, 20 (left), 22, 23 (right), 27, 29, 50, 48 (right), 28 (top right), 34 (left), 37 (right), 42 (bottom right), 43, 53 (left), 54 (right), 56 (bottom), 57 (top), 58, 68, 70, 78 (left), 80 (left), 116 (top), 148, 149 (bottom), 151 (top left), 154 (bottom), 162 (top right), 164 (left), 165 (right), 182, 184 (bottom), 187

Tim Peters: 15 (bottom), 41, 52 (bottom), 67 (bottom right), 71 (right), 77 (bottom), 83 (bottom right), 140 (bottom), 151 (bottom right), 153 (bottom), 160 (left), 165 (bottom right), 179 (bottom)

RIBA Collections: 16 (left), 49 (middle), 51, 64 (right), 91 (top), 109 (top), 127, 152 (top left), 157 (top); 27 (left) and 44 (bottom) – both John Maltby; 32, 65, 97 (top), 156 (top) – all Architectural Press Archive); 92 (left; Henk Snoek), 186 (bottom; Edwin Smith)

Alamy: 16 (right), 28 (left), 35, 62 (bottom right), 67 (left and top right), 105 (bottom right), 139, 150, 155, 159 (top), 160 (right), 164 (right), 172 (bottom), 174–6, 181

John Lewis Partnership Heritage Services: 17 (top), 76, 77 (top, bottom left), 108 (left), 128–30, 131 (right)

© Museum of London: 20 (right), 112 (left), 171

Graham Coster: 21, 135 (bottom), 137 (bottom), 157 (bottom)

Mieke Hille: 24 (right)

The Advertising Archives: 30

Shutterstock: 31, 151 (top right), 152 (bottom left), 179 (top)

Source: Historic England Archive: 33, 37 (left), 38 (right), 39, 40, 42 (top right), 47 (right), 71 (left), 99 (top), 148 (top), 158 (right), 160 (left)

Bishopsgate Institute: 34 (right), 61 (right)

Topfoto: 44 (top), 52 (top), 61 (left; *Punch* archive), 81

Look & Learn: 45 (bottom), 94 (bottom left), 146

Courtesy of Harrods Company Archive London: 53 (right)

Sarah J. Duncan: 55

© TfL from the London Transport Museum: 69

Wikicom: 74

Mirrorpix: 75, 166

Brighton Toy Museum: 80 (right), 83 (bottom left)

Bridgeman Art Library: 84

The Francis Frith Collection: 88 (left), 105 (top), 121, 126 (bottom)

Vestry House Museum, London Borough of Waltham Forest: 89

Dharam Sahdev: 90 (left)

Letterology.com: 98

Caroline Morris: 100 (right), 126 (bottom)

Joe Collier: 105 (bottom left)

© Martin Mayer/reportdigital.co.uk: 107

IanVisits: 108 (right)

Benedict O'Looney: 110–11

Swark Heritage: 112–3

Vivien Lovett: 122–4, 142 (top)

Wendy Easton: 125 (left)

Reproduced by kind permission of London Borough of Lambeth, Archives Department, lambethlandmark.com: 132–4, 136 (bottom), 137 (top)

House of Fraser Archive: 144 (left), 163 (top)

National Maritime Museum: 147

Royal Borough of Kensington & Chelsea: 159 (bottom), 173 (top and bottom left)

Tessa Boase: 162 (bottom right), 163 (bottom), 173 (bottom right)

Pamela Kingsford: 165 (left)

Squire & Partners (photography by James Jones): 177

Graham Turner, *Guardian* (eyevine.com): 180 (left)

PastRewind blog: 180 (right)